THE SPIRITUAL LIVES
OF DYING PEOPLE

THE SPIRITUAL LIVES OF DYING PEOPLE

Testimonies of Hope and Courage

Paul A. Scaglione
AND John M. Mulder

CASCADE *Books* · Eugene, Oregon

THE SPIRITUAL LIVES OF DYING PEOPLE
Testimonies of Hope and Courage

Original cover art: "Remembering" by Robert Kipniss. Used with permission.

Cascade Books
An Imprint of Wipf and Stock Publishers
199 W. 8th Ave., Suite 3
Eugene, OR 97401

www.wipfandstock.com

ISBN 13: 978-1-61097-772-2

Cataloguing-in-Publication data:

Scaglione, Paul A.

　　The spiritual lives of dying people : testimonies of hope and courage / Paul A. Scaglione and John M. Mulder.

　　xxii + 112 pp. ; 23 cm.

　　ISBN 13: 978-1-61097-772-2

　　1. Terminally ill—Pastoral counseling of. 2. Chaplains—Religious life. 3. Death—Religious aspects. I. Mulder, John M. II. Title.

R726.8 .S34 2013

Manufactured in the U.S.A.

Paul A. Scaglione dedicates this book
to the memory of my mother, Grace Marie Scaglione,
an example of deep, abiding faith
and
to the Gennesaret retreat teams in New Jersey and Kentucky
and all the Gennesaret retreatants.

John M. Mulder dedicates this book
to Robert L. Reed MD,
a physician who listens
and who saved our son's life.

CONTENTS

PREFACE

THIS BOOK IS THE product of a collaboration between two individuals who have become deep friends in the process of preparing it. Readers may wonder how it was actually written. The introduction was written by John M. Mulder, based on interviews with Paul A. Scaglione and participation in one of Father Paul's retreats for seriously ill people. The fifteen profiles of dying people were narrated by Paul and written up by John. The conclusion, which is an interview between Paul and John, speaks for itself. The names of people and their families who are described in this book have been changed to protect their anonymity.

In preparing this book for publication, we have been assisted in manifold ways by many people. Paul thanks Bob, Carol, Fr. Charlie, Sr. Ellen, Gordon, Hilare, Jerry, Mike, and Pat. John is especially grateful to his wife, Mary, an English composition professor, for reading the entire manuscript, and to his daughter Cora for reading many of the profiles. Their sharp eyes improved it immensely.

Though we come out of different communions, we know that nothing emerges without communities of support, and we give thanks to all those who have nurtured us and supported our endeavor to describe a few people who testified to their hope and courage as they made the last journey of life.

Paul A. Scaglione
John M. Mulder

INTRODUCTION

Paul: The Priest Who Listens

John M. Mulder

"Call me Paul."

So began our somewhat unlikely friendship—the Reverend Paul A. Scaglione, a Roman Catholic priest, and me, a Presbyterian minister. I was searching for "spiritual formation" from a "spiritual director." I quickly learned that Paul rejected the term "spiritual director" for "spiritual adviser"—my first indication of his humility and rejection of pretense. I needed spiritual formation and advice in the aftermath of a profound crisis in my life. I had crashed in my mid-fifties. I was killing my self—physically, emotionally, and spiritually. At the depth of my crash, counselors described me as "spiritually bankrupt" and afflicted with "a toxic level of shame and guilt."

Spiritual writer Mary Margaret Funk calls this *acedia*—"self-icide," not suicide. Paul Scaglione taught me to choose life, a new life—a new relationship with my self, my family, my friends, and God—all provided through God's grace and kindness and the forgiveness and love of people I had hurt.

Paul gave me a new life by listening to me. No other act better describes the heart of his ministry. At the end of our very first session, in which I talked incessantly, he asked me to meditate on these words from Psalm 46: "Be still and know that I am God."

In less than an hour, he had seen the heart of my problem—relentless work, manic achievement, constant expression. I could not shut up; that was my problem. I had spent my life and ministry speaking and writing. In truth, I was shuttered up, shut down, broken down. I had to shut up and listen—to God. I had to listen with my heart, attentive to God's faithful yet subtle direction. I had to develop *lev shomea* (Hebrew for "a listening heart").

As the years went by, our one-sided relationship—Paul listening, me talking—became reciprocal. I learned about him and his unusual ministry—the spiritual lives of dying people. It is a formal retreat ministry for the chronically ill, as well as Paul's personal mission as a pastor to accompany fellow believers at the end of their earthly journey. He listens to them, prays with them, and encourages them to listen to the movement of God in their transition. In doing so, he nurtures their ability to listen to themselves, to others, and to God.

Paul's gift of listening has been honed by his own life experience and has become the unique and surprising focus of his ministry. By listening, he helps people find God in the face of death. He is the listening priest.

It began in his own family. Paul was a chosen child. Born in 1947 in the wake of World War II, he was adopted by a childless Italian-American couple in New Jersey, Carmen and Grace Marie Scaglione. They subsequently adopted another child, Judy, and later Charlie was born into the family. "I always considered them my parents," he says. It was a conventional childhood for a Catholic kid raised in the midst of the postwar American religious revival—family, church, and Catholic school. His father owned a printing business with his brother. His mother was a homemaker, a gardener, and the center of their selected family and extended family. It was all very Italian and very Catholic.

In October 1966, when Paul was nineteen and a sophomore at Brescia University in Owensboro, Kentucky, tragedy struck the heart of his family. One day as his mother was engaged in fall housecleaning, she felt sick and lay down on her bed. Within an hour she was paralyzed from the waist down. She never walked again. From that fateful moment, her life changed permanently. Others would care for her basic needs. She had to be bathed and dressed. She never gardened outside her home again. And her spiritual life was never the same.

"I saw someone with a chronic illness," Paul recalls. "I saw the effect this has on a family. It played a major role in my decision to study for the priesthood. I bargained with God. 'God, if you will cure my mother, I will offer myself to you.'" He adds self-consciously, "I know that's pretty primitive, but it's true. I'm not there now."

His mother's illness consumed the family—her husband Carmen, her children, her siblings, her relatives and friends, and Johnson, a devoted African-American home health aide who cared for her for twenty-five years. Grace and her family stormed heaven with prayer that she would be restored to full health, walking again. In those early years of constant prayer she made handmade signs with one word: "WALK." The signs were all over the house, in every room. That was their hope. That was their prayer.

Paul finished Brescia University in 1968, graduating with a degree in political science. In his senior year he decided to enter seminary to pursue a process of vocational discernment for priesthood. He studied philosophy, Latin, and Greek at Mount Saint Paul Seminary in Waukesha, Wisconsin, for one year before entering Saint Meinrad Seminary in Saint Meinrad, Indiana. He graduated in 1973 from Saint Meinrad School of Theology and was ordained a Catholic priest on May 26, 1973, in the diocese of Trenton, New Jersey.

While in seminary, Paul confronted his own physical crisis. In January 1972 he participated in a travel seminar on Christian archeology in Rome. There he began to lose weight and suffered daily fatigue. His health continued to deteriorate. On March 17, 1972, he was ordained as a transitional deacon at Saint Meinrad Seminary. He returned to New Jersey and exercised his new ministry as a deacon during Holy Week, preaching for the first time on Easter Sunday morning. On Easter Monday, April 3, 1972, he awakened and could not lift his head from his pillow. He was rushed to the emergency room. His blood sugar had soared over eight hundred (normal is between seventy and one hundred). He drifted into a diabetic coma. After three and a half days, he woke up. The attending physician was astonished, and later that day, he told Paul, "There's no reason for your recovery. You were in the process of dying. I don't use this language, but this is a miracle."

Paul was astonished too. "I kept asking, 'Why, God? Why are you doing this to me, after all that I have promised to do for you?' That was my question. Eventually I developed a prayer. It was very simple. As I administered my morning dose of insulin, I thanked God for the gift of another day. I saw it as an opportunity serve in ways that God would make known to me."

As Paul continued his new ministry as a priest, his mother continued her spiritual journey as well. She surprised everyone in the family. When Paul returned home from his assignment at an inner-city parish in Trenton, he found that all the "WALK" signs were gone. He was shocked. He asked his Mom, "What have you done? Where are all the signs?" She replied simply, "I don't need them anymore." Paul responded, "You, all of us, have been praying for you to walk for more than seven years. I don't understand!"

His mother declared, "Paul, I learned that I have been praying for the wrong thing. I've been asking God to take me back to the past. As I prayed for what I wanted, I failed to see and know that God was here with me—as I am! My prayer used to be asking God to help me walk. Now my prayer is thanking God today for his presence in all of you who care for me. I am blessed and healed."

His mother's reaction to her own condition left an indelible mark on Paul's soul. "I learned," he concludes, "that you cannot be consumed by your need because it may block God from your life." And like his mother, Paul faced a future of chronic illness—diabetes. The doctor warned him he would die before he was sixty, but he foiled the doctor's prediction. "My fifty-ninth year was very difficult," he says. "I told no one. But reaching sixty was an amazing experience."

After his own confrontation with death, Paul returned to Saint Meinrad, received his degree, and was ordained to the priesthood. He was assigned as an associate pastor to the aforementioned inner-city church in Trenton—St. Joachim. It had two thousand households and a pastor who had served there for more than forty years. It was a traditional Catholic parish that lived in the world of the 1950s. "The people were wonderful, and their life stories beyond belief," Paul recalls. "It was a miracle St. Joachim's even existed," Paul jokes. "It was unique, to say the least."

His quiet and contagious spirituality quickly brought him back to Saint Meinrad. After only two years in the parish, Paul was appointed in 1975 as associate spiritual director and two years later as spiritual director for the entire seminary. He served eight years in a demanding environment in which vocations to the priesthood plummeted and seminarians wrestled with their callings. He earned a certificate in spirituality and spiritual direction in 1982 from the Institute for Spiritual Leadership in Chicago, affiliated with Loyola University. There he immersed himself in mystical theology, the Enneagram, and Jungian depth psychology. Paul plumbed the theology of Teilhard de Chardin and Thomas Merton and the meditations of the Spanish mystics, especially St. John of the Cross. The *via negativa* or "way of negation" of mystics resonated with his personal experience of God as mystery. "That is the most important part of my spiritual tradition," he says emphatically. "Their sense of mystery helped me deal with my mom's situation and my own physical condition. Why? Why? We can't understand these questions. Anselm said it was faith seeking understanding, but we can ask those questions only because God exists."

In 1985 he left Saint Meinrad, exhausted by the demands of his ministry of spiritual direction and formation. He was also desperately worried about his mother. His father had died in 1981, and his mother was now living alone. His brother, Charlie, was the primary family caregiver—until Charlie's job forced a move to North Carolina. Paul went home to take over the role of primary caregiver. It was 1985, and his mother would live in steadily declining health until 1998. For the next fourteen years, Paul served on the staff of two large suburban Catholic parishes, ten of those years as pastor, while continuing to coordinate care for his mother.

"Most of the week was consumed by the church ministry," he remembers. "But Mondays were for Mommy. Technically, it was my day off; in reality, it was my day to oversee her life, medical, financial, and home care issues." Her last years were very difficult and included three major surgeries. A full-time caregiver, Vicki from Guatemala, moved in. More than anything else, Paul says, "I was concerned about her being alone."

After her eightieth birthday and final surgery, Paul's mother entered a nursing home for one hundred days, was released, and died suddenly on the morning of July 7, 1998. At the same time, Paul found himself alone and sought therapy. He was also traumatized by the murder of a seven-year-old girl in his congregation. The boy who killed her was an orphan, adopted when he was three years old and abused. This tragedy triggered Paul's memories of his own sexual abuse by a priest when he was a young boy. "It was the lowest point of my life," Paul recalls. "It's remarkable that I made it. I was mainly angry at institutions—especially the church. I loved the people. I wished I could only have been a priest without being associated with the church."

While undergoing therapy, he had a breakthrough: "I discovered I could name my ministry in a personal way, instead of an ecclesiastical way. That was the key. The result was that I can absorb a lot of people's pain. I've learned that healing happens as you create a sacred space so people can tell their own story."

Early in his New Jersey pastorates, Paul met a remarkable woman, Hilare Reinold, at St. Benedict Church in Homdel. She was a homemaker and regularly attended daily Mass. She told Paul she liked to visit people who were sick at home. She also knew about Paul's mother and invited Paul to join her on her visits. Soon Paul began to accompany her to the homes of sick people in the congregation. "I was overwhelmed with how isolated they were," he remembers. "No one knew these people. They usually had few friends and no nearby caring family members."

Paul prayed about his visits and wondered if he and the church should be doing more. "Is this enough?" he asked God. "I stayed with that question." He listened for God's guidance, and as he listened, he worked. During his time at St. Benedict, Paul and the pastor, Father Bill Anderson, were on call 24/7 at the local hospital as well, ministering to dying people and their families. "It was a baptism by fire," Paul says. "I was absorbed by it. I loved it. I could have done it for the rest of my life."

Through Hilare Reinold, Paul met a woman who had inoperable stomach cancer. She was divorced and had not remarried—and was alienated from her family. She lived in a tiny bungalow in a blue-collar neighborhood. She went in and out of the hospital, and her only care came from neighbors and friends—plus Hilare and Paul. The day she died in the hospital, she was surrounded by a nurse, the hospital chaplain, and Paul. They held vigil by her bedside, holding her hands and praying and crying with her. She was waiting for a visit from an estranged son, but he never came.

At the end, "it felt right," Paul says. "She died, but at her death she had a deep confidence that God was with her. God was her strength and anchor. She trusted God. The moment of her death was completion. You could see it on her face. God transformed her suffering and took it upon himself."

But Paul later found he was angry. "I felt lonely because of her loneliness, and I was mad that she was alone. I was angry that she had been neglected for whatever reason by her son. It convinced me that no one should die alone and forgotten."

The home pastoral care visitations in the parish continued, but Paul persisted in asking Hilare, "Is this enough?" They began to explore a ministry to people isolated by illness. Paul was transferred to a new parish, his first pastorate at St. Thomas More Church in Manalpan, New Jersey, but he continued pursuing this idea with Hilare. Together they called friends and professionals to share their concern and open a process for prayerful discernment. Over several weeks, they prayed and searched the Scriptures, all the while seeking God's direction. The discussions were exhaustive and many options were explored. But Paul urged patience and refused to implement something immediately. He waited. He listened. "I gave it time," he says.

One alternative was the hospice model, but Paul envisioned something different. He wanted to support people in their illness and prepare them for their death. "Suffering in itself has no meaning," he says. "It's fruitless to get into the question, 'Why did this happen?' Instead, I wanted to help people understand the meaning of suffering in their lives. I wanted to help them answer the question, 'Where is God in this?' I wanted to help them understand that God knew the burden of their suffering and would embrace it with them. This was the liberation of the cross. It wasn't just about the forgiveness of sins."

What emerged was the notion of a spiritual retreat for people with chronic or life-threatening illnesses; Paul and his colleagues call it the Gennesaret Retreat for the Seriously Ill, using Mark 6:53–57 as their scriptural inspiration. They have settled on a three-day model—from Friday to midday on Sunday. The retreat focuses on listening to God, seeking the voice of God in prayer, conversation, liturgies, and group meetings. "There are no jobs and no tasks—except one, to receive the grace of God's word spoken to them during this sacred time," says Paul.

Paul and the retreat team had much hard work to do to implement this vision. From the beginning, there were enormous logistical obstacles. The candidates for the retreat needed medical care and equipment. They were invariably strapped financially—and isolated. They saw their homes as their primary security, so they had to be reassured of their safety and comfort on the retreat. "Going on a retreat is a threat," Paul says. "We have to alleviate the stress of that anxiety."

The result: Gennesaret Retreats are free. They are open to anyone with a chronic, life-threatening illness (non-Catholics and even some Jews have participated). Full nursing care, medical equipment, and medical care are provided. For a retreat of ten to twelve "guests," as they are called, a staff of twenty to twenty-five is needed, including at least ten nurses. All are volunteers. A registered nurse does a health history and medical assessment of every prospective guest before the retreat. Paul follows up with a personal spiritual assessment.

After twenty-five years, nearly a thousand guests have experienced a Gennesaret Retreat in Catholic dioceses primarily in the Northeast and in the archdiocese of Louisville, Kentucky.

On the retreat, there is one surprising prohibition—no talk about being sick. "The ill are self-absorbed by their illnesses," Paul maintains. "The whole intention of our retreats is to help them to listen to God speaking through others and in their own hearts. Our goal is to open their hearts to listen and receive whatever God desires to give them."

The guests are truly ill. For example, one typical retreat involved sixteen guests, ranging in age from forty-nine to eighty-eight. Their conditions included brain tumor surgery (with postoperative mood swings and depression), multiple diagnoses of cancer (colon, bladder, skin, lung, chest wall), chronic and progressive multiple sclerosis (with rods and pins in one leg), severe degenerative rheumatoid arthritis, stroke, cardiac bypass surgery, valve replacement, aortic graft replacement, osteoporosis, cancer of the stomach, breast cancer, epilepsy, cerebral aneurysm, diabetes, kidney transplant, spinal birth defect, fractured hip, heart valve disease, and a pacemaker implant.

The list of "special needs" for these guests is overwhelming. For example: "uses walker at all times and wears back brace," "generalized weakness; dietary needs, doesn't eat meat," "very emotional and sensitive and suffers some depression," "must use oxygen at all times," "has had problems with falls—needs assistance with stairs," "always uses walker and needs wheelchair for distances," "tires very easily—symptoms of numbness and exhaustion are increasing," "has difficulty with gait," "constant assistance with personal needs and hygiene," "generalized weakness and depression," "balance difficulties," "legally blind," "is unable to sit up for long periods," and "tires easily due to heart disease and aging."

The retreat begins in the early afternoon on Friday. Paul gives a presentation in which he emphasizes listening as the focus of their time together. He urges them to spend time alone or with others—listening. He passes out cards to each guest. "Write what is on your heart," he tells them. "What do you bring to God, what need or prayer as you begin this retreat?" Each prayer card is placed in a bowl that is present through the retreat conferences and prayer services.

In the late afternoon, the Eucharist is celebrated, followed by dinner. Then Paul talks about the day ahead and suggests that as they say their prayers that night, they consider Philippians 4:13: "I can do all things through him who strengthens me." "We're very strong on Scripture," he says, "but we're not directive about it. Scripture can speak in so many ways through so many texts. But we have to listen to hear it."

The guests go to their rooms. The staff meet for much-needed prayer. The night watch begins. There is always someone walking the halls, attentive to anyone in need.

After breakfast on Saturday, Paul briefly talks to the guests about the meaning of the cross and gives each guest a small crucifix. He quotes Pope

John XXIII: "The greatest challenge of the spiritual life is not to give love but receive love." Paul tells them, "God wants to give you something, but your fear is a big issue. God loves you as you are. You do not need to change, but you do need to be willing to receive. Our inability to receive is tied to our inability to listen, which impedes our ability to understand God's will for us. Each of us builds ironclad walls, which we don't even see. Push your distractions aside and let grace work. We see life as a series of events. That's 'time' for us. But God has no 'time.' God is always with us."

In the second half of the morning, guests receive a healing blanket prayerfully made by a supporting parish community. Paul invites the guests to reflect on the cross as a living symbol of God's union with them in their suffering. Their suffering is known by God and embraced by God as a place of hope and victory. The vertical and horizontal lines of the cross reflect one's personal relationship with God and the living witness of God through others. The cross is the sign of victory over the moment of death, Paul says, as well as the promise of eternal life in the company of God and the community of saints.

After breaking for lunch and a rest period, the guests reconvene. Then follows what Paul has called "the most powerful experience of my life." Paul assembles everyone for a time of solemn prayer called the adoration of the Blessed Sacrament. Gathered in the chapel, the guests sit in a circle surrounded by the retreat staff. Before everyone on the altar sits a small monstrance, or gold frame, containing a consecrated host (wafer). The Scriptures are read recalling God's covenant of love for his people. Roman Catholics believe that in the celebration of the Eucharist, the bread and the wine become the "real presence" of Jesus Christ. The living sacramental presence of Jesus is reserved in the tabernacles of Catholic churches for distribution to the sick and dying and for prayerful adoration. This service is one of adoration. Father Paul carries the small monstrance to each guest, who is given time to pray with Jesus for as long as he or she needs as the retreat team sings softly in the background. As they pray, these seriously ill people connect with Jesus, the One who promises to be with them always, to love them without end. "The silence of that service is charged with holiness," says Paul.

After a period of rest, Paul celebrates the Eucharist again in the late afternoon. Dinner follows, and the closing ritual of the day is the sacrament of the Anointing of the Sick. In this sacrament, the community of faith—the church—prays for the recovery of the sick and peaceful transition of the dying to the company of God. The anointing reaffirms the promise of God that whenever the church prays and exercises a healing ministry in the name of the Lord, God will raise up the sick persons and save them. Members of the retreat team are offered an opportunity to receive this sacrament as well.

The day ends with "Gaudeamus" (Latin for "let's rejoice"). This is a continuation of the prayerful gatherings of the day. Now the guests are treated to a program of joyous songs, wonderful food, and abundant laughter. After a long day of conferences and prayer services, all the retreat participants and retreat staff "enjoy gathering for fun, a time to laugh and sing and to recognize that God is in all things!" says Paul.

On Sunday morning after breakfast, Paul invites the guests to take time alone and review what has happened on the retreat. They are encouraged to name a moment, conversation, prayer, or word they received from God during the retreat. After a period alone, the guests come back together. They are offered the opportunity to speak about their experience, though some choose to remain silent. These reflections are shared without comment; they are received with compassion and thanksgiving to God. At the end of this shared reflection, each guest is invited to take one of the prayer cards home with them and to continue to pray for the guest who wrote it at the beginning of the retreat. The gathering ends with staff washing and anointing the feet of the guests. This ritual of honor and respect for the guests captures the spirit of the retreat. With this final action, the guests and staff go to the chapel to welcome family members for Sunday Eucharist, and later a closing lunch for all.

The retreat is an elegantly simple idea: a time of silence so that seriously ill people can listen. They can prayerfully listen and receive the consolation of God's presence in this stage of life. And in listening, they hear the deepest longings of their own hearts. They receive. They find God.

One example: a woman with terminal cancer registered for a Genneseret Retreat. A week before the retreat, she suddenly cancelled. When the next retreat came up, she registered again. When she arrived, she was defensive and sullen. Eventually she asked Paul if she could speak with him during one of the quiet times. When they met, she told her story—at first slowly and then in a torrent of words. Her husband sexually abused her. Her priest had told her to keep the marriage together despite the abuse. She finally divorced her husband. She had an adopted son, and just before she attended the retreat, he told his mother he was HIV positive.

It was the first time in her life she had disclosed to anyone the pain of her life. Paul said nothing. He listened. At the end, she said, "You are the first priest or even the first human being who has listened to me without comment and without judgment." And then she cried.

"People want to be received with care," Paul says. "By listening to ourselves, we receive. By listening to others, we receive. By listening to God, we receive. Listening is so difficult for us. But it is the way we hear the deepest longings of our hearts and the loving words of God."

"The message of God comes in a thousand different voices," Paul declares.

At the end of one Gennesaret Retreat, when Paul was clearly drained, I asked him, "Why do you do these retreats?" He replied, "This is what I am meant to do."

This book contains the voices of a few of those who showed in their dying how they learned to listen and receive the loving embrace of God. At the end of their lives and in their own unique and different ways, they found God—with the help of a priest who listened.

MARIA

The Woman Who Yearned for Reconciliation

I MET MARIA IN the early 1990s while I was serving as pastor of a large, suburban congregation with more than three thousand households. During one Lenten season, I offered to pray with anyone who wanted intercessory prayer immediately after Mass.

One Sunday Maria stopped me in the middle of the foyer. She told me forcefully, "I need a prayer for my medical condition." "Now?" I asked. "Yes, now," she insisted. "Why?" I inquired. "Because I have a hard decision to make. I need some help."

I asked her to explain her situation before we started to pray. She reported that she was a survivor of breast cancer. She had undergone surgery six years earlier, and her cancer went into remission. But now it had reappeared, and she didn't know what treatment she should undergo.

I placed my hands on her shoulders, and she put her hands around me. I prayed in a whisper that she would be aware of and be filled with the presence and wisdom of God to recognize the possibilities that were unfolding for her. She prayed for strength to endure and handle the chaos of her inner life. A madhouse of people was swirling all around us in the foyer, but we paid no attention to them. Her husband stood in the background.

That first encounter symbolized what eventually became one of the most extraordinary spiritual relationships of my ministry. Maria was an Italian-American woman in her late fifties with equal parts humble piety and strong will. She had four children, all living away from home; her husband owned a business in New York City; and as mother and wife, she was the center, the glue of her family's life (this is true in many Italian families). She yearned for God's presence and guidance, but she also took responsibility for her life—her treatment for cancer and her accountability with others and with God.

After that prayer in the foyer, Maria consulted with her doctor and later called me to come to her home. She reported that the cancer had spread to her lymph nodes, and the doctor recommended chemotherapy. Keenly aware of her condition, she was shocked by the reappearance of the cancer. Nevertheless, she said, "I think I don't have enough information to make a good decision." She decided on a second opinion, and it came back the same. Both doctors suggested chemotherapy sooner rather than later.

She received eight chemotherapy treatments over the next couple of months. To virtually everyone, she appeared very upbeat. "God is with me," she told me. "I have the support of you and my family and friends." She had high energy and retained a positive image of herself. There was no fear, no anger. But there were low spots—witnessed only by her husband.

After three months and more tests, Maria learned that the cancer was spreading, and this time the doctors recommended radiation. She agreed. Again, she took charge of her treatment and her outward behavior, but this time she suffered many more side effects, including fatigue and loss of hair. She withdrew inside herself and came to Mass only occasionally. People began to ask about her. I knew more than anyone, including her children, but I told people, "She needs some time for herself."

Whenever she called, I visited her at home. She would call me whenever she needed an ear, often to vent about her doctors. During these visits, I did a good deal of pastoral counseling, but we did not do much praying.

After several months of radiation, she showed dramatic improvement and then started a rigorous cycle of treatment—radiation, then chemotherapy, followed by more radiation and chemotherapy—lasting more than six months. For the first time, she asked, "What do you think God wants me to do with this?" I responded, "What do you mean?" She said, "Does God have a plan for my treatment? Shall I continue it or stop it?"

I told her, "I don't know the mind of God—never known it, never will know it."

Maria said, "I believe God has a plan for my treatment, but I can't know it for sure." She asked me to pray for her that God would give her wisdom to know God's will.

"Prayer alone is not enough," I said. "We need to have conversations to discern God's will." I left it with her to call me back.

After a couple of weeks, she called. When we met at her home, she said, "I keep asking, 'Is this God's will or my will?' I think I've decided it's my will when the choices involve control and purpose—something visible and tangible. And it's God's will when the choices are open-ended. I think God's telling me, 'I am with you. I just want you to fall back into my arms.'" Then she asked me to pray, and I asked God for perspective—to give Maria the wisdom to understand how her will and God's will were intertwined.

Following this dramatic spiritual insight, she endured more tests and chemotherapy, and then she received word: remission. Now her fighter instincts returned. She was in charge. "I'm going to beat this," she told me. "I won."

All the talk about God ended. I wondered where this was going. I had so many questions, but I didn't discuss them with her.

The remission lasted more than a year and a half. But one day after Sunday Mass, she came to me in the foyer again—same place, same time, with the same prayer for discernment. The cancer had returned, and this time it was a very invasive form of cancer, affecting not only the lymph nodes but other parts of her body as well. The doctors recommended an aggressive course of chemotherapy. I prayed that God would grant her discernment to know the right path.

This time she decided to fight on her own and chose a program of alternative medicine. She went into it aggressively with vitamins and a new diet of herbs and health foods. She went full speed ahead into this attack on her disease. It was as if she was saying, "I beat this with surgery. Then I beat it with chemotherapy and radiation. Now I'm going to prove the doctors are wrong and beat it by myself."

She convinced her family. "There's no way in hell this will beat her," they told me. "She'll beat anything under the sun. She knows better than her doctors how to handle her disease." To my surprise, she went into remission.

As her spiritual counselor, I noticed she stopped talking about God and God's guidance to give her wisdom. I found this very disconcerting. I never said this to her, but I thought that if the cancer reappeared, the battle would be nastier than anything she had ever seen. It would be the end of her life.

During this period of alternative medicine, she would stop me after Sunday Mass. We talked about her cooking and other day-to-day matters. We did not meet regularly. Everything seemed satisfactory.

But then the cancer returned, and this time it was in the early stages of metastasis. She was completely and absolutely devastated. And so we had another prayer moment in the foyer of the church. I prayed that God would give her the courage and strength to listen to her doctor. She called me immediately after her consultation with the doctor, who had recommended treatment with a highly experimental drug currently in clinical trials. They spoke on Friday, and the doctor told her he had to know by Monday if she was interested.

We met on Sunday afternoon. Maria was totally miserable and very depressed. She was angry with God, with her husband, and with herself. She was all over the place. Her opening line to me was, "I can't fight this anymore."

At this point her husband emerged from his quietude and told Maria that he loved her very much and wanted her to know that he was her faithful companion for whatever might lie ahead. He would be with her no matter what. I was moved by his wisdom and love for her. His affirmation of her quelled the distress and depression in her heart and soul. The next day she called with her decision: no more treatment. "I wanted you to know," she said. "Now is the time for me 'to prepare myself to meet the One who loves me,' and I am counting on your help."

I was astounded. I feared that she believed God had abandoned her. Her affirmation of preparing to meet God face to face touched my soul. It was the first time anyone had told me this. I burst into tears.

A few days later, she said, "I need your help in this process. I want you to pray with me. I want you to be with me when I pray. I don't want to do this alone."

"What about your husband?" I asked.

"No, I don't want to burden him with anything more."

This was the beginning of my extraordinary prayer sessions with Maria. When I would arrive at her home, I would go to her bedroom. She was dressed and ready, sitting in one of two chairs placed side by side.

At the first session, I pressed her to explain what she actually wanted me to do. She declared, "I can't do this unless someone else is listening to me. Things in my life are not settled. I need to go into a new territory. I need to say it out loud." She said she wanted to be honest enough "so I can meet God. Otherwise, he'll see right through me." She continued, "I can do this if you will be here with me."

We met weekly in the late afternoons or Saturday mornings. Sometimes she sent her husband away. We held hands.

Here's what she did. She went methodically through every relationship with every person in her family—alive or dead—covering all kinds of unresolved issues. In many of these incidents, she had been mean or cruel. She started with her mother, then her father, then her siblings, other members of her family, and some friends. She described these events in unbelievable detail.

She led; I followed as her prayer companion. I never prayed aloud, but silently I asked God that she would trust me. And she did trust me. She told me about some painful things she had done. She had willed them and she knew it. That kind of exposure really surprised me. All I could do was listen. It was almost like watching Maria talk to someone on the other side. It was an actual conversation with God and the person she hurt. She did it all. She wanted reconciliation, and she knew it was up to her. It was as if she had decided, "Death is my last choice."

As Maria weakened, she said her prayers from her bed. I sat on the bed, holding her hand. Sometimes her husband sat at the foot of the bed. The prayers began with silence, and then she would start to speak in a stream of consciousness. "What I feel in my heart is this," she would say. "I can't meet you until I make peace." For example, she described her relationship with an older sister, who had died many years earlier. "We never really connected," she said. "We competed for attention. There was a chasm between us. I never knew my sister." And then she added, "I don't want to meet her with all these barriers between us."

This hardworking, resilient, Italian-American mother with no formal education beyond high school showed me her intuitive understanding of good mental health—born out of her spiritual life. I began to see that I represented the church—the presence of God in her life. I was not prepared for this at all. It wasn't counseling. I did not probe. I did not process her feelings. It was her journey—a moral inventory. She was a prayer warrior.

During the last two months of her life, we met about six times for an hour. Each time the meeting was totally guided by her. Sometimes she would elaborate on her feelings; sometimes she would speak very simply. She never used any notes. She was never repetitive. She never asked for pardon. All she wanted from me was to be with her as she walked the road, owning and taking responsibility for her life.

Near the end of her life, I asked Maria to carry something to God for me. I told her, "I want my ministry to dying people to be the focus of all that I do." She said she would tell God, and I trust that she did.

She died just before sunrise at about 8 A.M. on a Saturday. Her bedroom had windows above her bed; the sun broke in at the moment of her death. Her husband was there. There's an old Italian proverb: "The person who goes quietly, goes with health and goes far." So it was with Maria. Her death was very peaceful. She simply stopped breathing.

I learned an enormous amount from Maria. It was the most profound experience of my ministry. Nothing comes close to it.

I learned that even though I felt very close to Maria, the process of dying is so powerful and personal that someone else can't feel the intimacy. The last journey was all hers, not mine. I could have run one hundred kilometers around her bed, but she had to run the race alone. Her moral inventory—her prayers of reconciliation—taught me that we sometimes think we have so much time, but in reality, all we have is now—each day, each hour—to live with God and others and find restoration.

Death is a sacred space. I really don't know what dying is all about. I can't know exactly what it is, and I don't have a clue. I can have my head on a person's chest—be that close—and still not know.

All I can do is help people fall into the mystery of faith. Death is falling backwards into the arms of the ultimate mystery of God—the reality of love.

It was easy to celebrate her funeral Mass. I still feel connected with her. We have a relationship beyond death. I'm a much better priest because of Maria. I am much more sensitive to people and their dying. As best as any human being can do, I learned what it means to be reconciled with God and with others. From Maria, I learned what it means to prepare to meet God.

I know Maria is part of the communion of saints.

It was my privilege—and a blessing from God—to know a saint.

Reflection

Maria's journey was a determined effort to set things right before meeting God face to face. In her heart she carried regrets, broken promises, and barriers of all sorts. The weight of her life experiences needed to be lifted from her heart so that she could meet the One who loved her. Her last days were filled with honesty and prayerful surrender in the company of her family, whose love was her strength.

Prayer

God, please keep us honest and hopeful in our journey home. Give us wisdom and confidence in your forgiving love, and keep us aware of all that we must surrender in order to meet you face to face. May your love encourage us with the gift of peaceful surrender and grant us joyful reunion with you. Amen.

BEN

The Man Who Could Have Been a Monk

I RETURNED TO KENTUCKY in the late 1990s. It was a big transition for me. I had buried my mother and sold the family home in 1998. After two and a half years of struggle over whether to remain a priest because of my childhood sexual abuse by a priest and other issues that surfaced during therapy, I decided to leave the diocese of Trenton in New Jersey. There I left behind a large suburban parish community of thirty-two hundred households and more than twelve thousand people where I had been pastor. At my new parish in Kentucky, I was an associate pastor again. I was number three in seniority on the staff behind the pastor and senior associate priest. I knew absolutely no one.

One of the good things about my new assignment was that I enjoyed a lot of free time. In my homilies, I began to mention the spiritual retreats I had developed in New Jersey. I described them as a time for people with chronic or serious illnesses to reflect on the presence of God in their lives. Two people immediately latched on to the idea. At my invitation these two parishioners went to New Jersey to experience the retreat firsthand. They came back enthused. Their leadership and organizational skills became the driving force that gathered a nucleus of volunteers for the retreats. After showing my concern for the sick, I began to receive calls from parishioners who were seriously ill. I met with them initially for sacramental ministry, primarily the Anointing of the Sick. Gradually, I felt that I had found my niche in ministry again.

Ben was one of the first people I met. A short, stout, balding man in his early sixties, Ben had been diagnosed with liver cancer but looked good for his age and condition. He was retired from working for an automaker, and he and his wife Mary had recently moved to the Louisville area to be near their only daughter and grandson. His father had also spent his life-time working for an automaker, and because of that family legacy, Ben was especially fond of an old Buick that he had brought with him from Michigan and was now stored in his garage.

I had met Ben and Mary several times after Mass. Mary was very pleasant and gracious and always talked for the two of them. Ben would stand slightly behind her and say nothing. Mary eventually called and told me that Ben needed me. When someone calls in behalf of someone else, my antennae go up because I don't know who really needs ministry. Mary was very anxious and verbose, hardly giving me a chance to respond during her nonstop recitation of Ben's needs. I'm always alarmed when I hear someone tell me what someone else's needs are.

I agreed to visit with them in their home. They had bought a modest patio home near the church, and when I pulled up in front of the house, I paused because I was unsure whether to park in the driveway or in front of the house. Mary immediately came outside and directed me into the drive-way. Now this is a terrible thing to say about someone I barely knew, but the thought ran through my head, "Oh God, I know who's in control here."

When I entered the house, Ben was sitting in a lounge chair on the sunporch at the front of their home—his favorite place, as I later learned. Mary immediately sat down next to him. My first impression was that if this gentleman had a lot to say about his illness and impending death, it was being overwhelmed by his wife. I decided to move slowly during this first visit by using the sacramental rituals for Anointing of the Sick and Holy Communion. All three of us prayed together and then began to talk. I asked Ben about his life. Ben spoke briefly about his background, the move from Michigan, and his illness. I asked him if he would like me to come again, and he said he would like that very much.

I promised to visit, and as I left I thanked Mary for the opportunity to visit and added that I hoped that Ben would feel more comfortable talking about his illness. I suggested that Ben and I probably needed some time alone. She agreed, and on subsequent visits she graciously welcomed me to their home and after a few minutes together excused herself so that we could be alone. I knew that she was concerned and even worried about what he was saying, or more importantly, not saying. As I gained her trust, her anxiety decreased, and eventually she stopped asking, "How did it go today?"

Ben and Mary were studies in contrast. Ben was very quiet and re-served. When I engage someone like this, I never know what it means. I am now wise enough to know that everyone reveals his or her story slowly, and patience is a virtue practiced over and over again by listening with your heart. Sometimes a quiet reserve can signal resistance or a lack of trust, but with Ben it was contentment and comfort, a kind of inner peace. He was introspective, a natural contemplative—a monk who was never a monk.

On the other hand, Mary was a case study in anxiety. She talked rap-idly and incessantly. She had a very traditional piety, consisting of regular rosary devotions and novenas. Over the course of my relationship with Ben, she kept on praying for a miracle and pressed me with materials about miraculous healing. Above all, she kept on insisting that Ben needed to talk to a priest about his cancer, but when the three of us were together, she did nearly all the talking and always referred to Ben in the third person—as if he wasn't there.

After my first visit, Ben and I met alone, and he unfolded his life story. He told me that his liver cancer had been diagnosed three years earlier. He underwent chemotherapy treatments, and he reported simply, "I do what they tell me to do." He talked about selling their old home in Michigan, moving to Louisville, and being near his daughter and grandson. Since he had stopped driving, he now felt immobile and isolated. He knew the way to the church and to his daughter's house and grandson's house. "I know maybe two other people," he said. He missed gardening, a favorite hobby, especially because the grounds of their patio home were maintained by a homeowners' association. He compensated by watching the groundskeeper work and by caring for several houseplants on the sunporch.

"I am at peace with this—my disease. I'm going to die," he told me. His real anxiety was his concern about the impact of his death on his wife, his daughter, and his grandson, with whom he shared a very close bond. "I want to live mostly for my grandson," he said, adding that he really missed fishing with him. "While I worry about Mary and my daughter, that's not where I'm invested. I'd like to spend more years with him."

Ben, the contemplative, was someone who was very honest about his disease and knew it would result in his death. He was very cooperative with his doctors. He was at peace with his disease and with meeting God. He didn't put much stock in his wife's prayers for "a miracle," he told me, and what he couldn't handle was his wife's anxiety. "I find it so tiring to listen to her," he said, "so sometimes I quote Scripture to her: 'Be not afraid.' That works, but not for long."

I gradually learned about something else that weighed on Ben's mind: he had lost touch with his brothers and sisters. When Ben's mother was dying, Ben and Mary moved her into their home, and Mary provided care for her until she died. I could feel the pain in his heart as he described the estrangement with his siblings. Whatever occurred during this caregiving for Ben's mother, whether intentional or unintentional, it created a division in the family. Ben and Mary were estranged from Ben's siblings, and the resentment and hurt stretched throughout the family. While Ben battled his cancer in Louisville, only one of his siblings called. None visited. Ben suffered from a sad and painful grief. And when he died, only one brother came to the funeral.

That was the only note of regret I ever heard from Ben. But I soon realized that our times together on the sunporch were sacred times for him. That was his sacred space. As our conversations continued, Ben talked more freely about his life, his dreams about his grandson's future, his regrets, and his hopes. He did not let his disease control his life. He dealt with it directly while understanding that life was not a survival contest; it was a journey back to God. His impending death did not frighten him. He said to me, "I know that death is simply the last step in my journey home to God. I want to make that step with confidence in Him."

Ben began to go downhill rapidly after our first few months of conversations. He had hospital admissions for pneumonia and renal failure and received transfusions. While he was in the hospital, he was usually heavily medicated and asleep or able to communicate only briefly. I prayed with him, sometimes asking his family for time alone. On one of his last hospitalizations, he asked that I pray for two things: first, for strength to endure his suffering and death, and second, for a sense of consolation and peace for his wife, his daughter, and his grandson. He never asked for prayers for his siblings.

Seven months after I met him, Ben died. I wasn't present at his death, but I visited with him twice during the last four days of his life. When he was close to dying, the family called me. Hospice had been called in, and he was nonresponsive. I anointed him again and prayed quietly for a peaceful journey home to God. His death was very hard on Mary; she was in shock and disbelief. She wasn't prepared for that fatal moment, and grief overwhelmed her.

During that last visit, I broached the subject of Ben's funeral with Mary and their daughter. Mary was still in denial about Ben's death and said she had made no plans. I worked with his daughter and grandson and the parish bereavement committee on the plans for Ben's funeral Mass. It included his grandson's reading one of the Scripture selections.

After the funeral, Mary praised me effusively. She said, "You walk on water." She showered me with gifts, both then and later, and she said repeatedly, "You were there for us." Ironically, I may have helped Mary by creating some distance between Ben and her. In retrospect, I can see that I put myself between them and perhaps reduced Mary's anxiety, which threatened to envelop both of them. It created a sacred space for Ben as well, even though he had been preparing himself for his death for a long time before I met him. He was confident in God's mercy. He knew it was time for him to die.

But the anxiety of his wife and daughter was stressful for him. He worried about how they would deal with his death. He was also afraid of the family tension between him and his siblings over their mother's death. "Did we do the right thing?" he would ask. When I reassured him of God's love, I asked him to surrender his doubt to God and trust God's mercy. He said, "Then I hope and pray that God's mercy will flow over all of us."

I wish I had had one more conversation with Ben before he died. Frequently, when a person is near death, I speak to them quietly—one on one—but in Ben's case that conversation never happened. On my last visit, just the day before he died, I remember whispering in his ear, "Leave your anxiety about everyone in your family behind. Don't hold on. Let go. God is waiting." Ben did let go, and he found God waiting for him.

St. Benedict, the founder of monasticism, said, "Listen and attend with the ear of your heart."

In so many ways, Ben instinctively knew that. He had received the gift of knowing how to listen. He attended to God with the ear of his heart. While others about him feared his death, he was not afraid. He feared only their anxiety and loss when he died.

He was a contemplative who had never lived in a monastery, and yet he knew how to contemplate the mystery of God's love and to rejoice in it.

He died in peace, hoping that his loved ones would know the peace he had found.

Reflection

The challenges of living through the last stages of a terminal illness are daunting. It is a daily struggle to claim a direction for your soul journey to God amid the compelling voices of loved ones, doctors, family, and professional caregivers. For Ben, what remained was his grief over what will not be. Grief laden with anxiety is toxic; for a contemplative soul, it is painful beyond measure. It is love scarred by past events and burdened by time running out. As Ben slowly surrendered his grief and anxiety to God, his peace grew. It was his final gift to the family he loved.

Prayer

Lord, free us from the anxiety of our unfinished lives. Let us trust that you will bring to completion all that we hope for in this life. Let us surrender our grief and worries to you one step at a time—one person, one memory, one dream at a time. Let your peace become our final gift to our loved ones, so that in you we all may be secure. Amen.

SARAH

The Woman Who Had Questions

S ARAH ATTENDED ONE OF our autumn spiritual retreats for people who are seriously ill. These Gennesaret Retreats are named after the region where Jesus carried out most of his ministry. They are held at the Abbey of Gethsemani near Bardstown, Kentucky, the Trappist monastery made famous by Thomas Merton, who lived and worked there for many years. My relationship with Sarah was short and intense. Six months after I met her, she died.

Her participation in the retreat was somewhat unusual. Sarah was not actively involved in the Catholic community, although she had been baptized and raised as a Catholic. She heard about the retreat through a friend who saw an ad about it in a parish bulletin. Sarah's illness was pancreatic cancer. That form of cancer usually brings death within a year, but amazingly she had survived for more than three years. Sarah met with the retreat nurse coordinator, who did a medical history and evaluation that determined she was healthy enough to participate in the retreat.

I did the spiritual evaluation of her life situation, her relationship with her illness and with God, and the anxieties that might inhibit her from receiving and hearing what we offer on the retreat. I always try to do these spiritual assessments in person, but because of miscommunication, Sarah and I missed an appointment at a local coffee shop. I called her with an apology and offered another time to meet with her to do the spiritual assessment. She declined. She insisted that a phone interview was sufficient, and in it she set the direction of our conversation. From the very beginning, it was evident that this was a woman who was in control.

She was an unmarried woman in her fifties. She was very matter-of-fact about her disease. Her mother had died a year earlier, and she had assumed full care for her mother during her mother's final years. She claimed initially that she had no problem doing that, though I later learned she struggled being her mother's primary caregiver. She had three sisters and two brothers, but it was Sarah alone who provided her mother with total care. In the course of nursing her mother, she realized that her own health was deteriorating. For the last two years of her mother's life, Sarah knew she had pancreatic cancer. She did not let her illness interfere with her caregiving; she stoically carried the burden. Later she would tell me that her mother's death was a somber path to follow as she lived with her own fatal disease.

When I asked whether she had ever been on a retreat, she reported that she had been on only one, as a very young girl. When I asked her about her faith, she flatly replied, "I have more questions than answers." As I later learned, that brusque comment spoke volumes about Sarah. She was a skeptic. I sensed that she had been alienated and estranged from God and the church, but I didn't know why. Gradually, I learned that she was searching—for answers, but also love.

At the retreat, we had several people who were very verbal, but Sarah was quiet, guarded, and introspective. She was clearly reflective but not comfortable sharing herself. When the talkative ones insisted that everyone should introduce him or herself, she announced that she had a terminal illness. Nothing more.

I eventually discovered that Sarah had always managed her own businesses. She described herself as an entrepreneur. She had successfully started and sold a couple of companies that imported and distributed cosmetics—a field she knew. She had no training in business, and she said she kept her business plans in her head. She was a manager—of her businesses and of her life.

Two things had an enormous impact on her during the retreat. The first came when I quoted Pope John XXIII: "The greatest challenge of the spiritual life is not to love but to receive love." That disturbed her because she felt that this had never been part of her life. The idea of *receiving* love really hit her.

The second was when she picked up a card in the monastery's retreat center on which was printed this famous prayer by Thomas Merton:

> My Lord God, I have no idea where I am going. I do not see the road ahead of me. I cannot know for certain where it will end. Nor do I really know myself, and the fact that I think I am following

your will does not mean that I am actually doing so. But I believe the desire to please you does in fact please you. And I hope I have that desire in all that I am doing. I hope that I will never do anything apart from that desire. And I know that if I do this you will lead me by the right road, though I may know nothing about it. Therefore will I trust you always though I may seem to be lost and in the shadow of death. I will not fear, for you are ever with me, and you will never leave me to face my perils alone.[1]

I had no conversations with Sarah until the last day of the retreat when she asked to meet with me. At that meeting, she told me about Merton's prayer and especially the quotation from Pope John XXIII. She declared, "I don't know if God can love me. A lot in my life is unlovable."

In my typical, somewhat no-holds-barred style, I replied, "It's not your choice; it's God's. It's God's will to love you as you are."

Sarah replied, "I've struggled with that all my life."

Then she began to tell her story. The burden of caring for her mother had left her "stretched out." She had been a caregiver while at the same time having to care for herself. She was never sure whether she was meeting her mother's needs, and now was plagued by the fact that the first anniversary of her mother's death was approaching.

I asked her, "How is your disease for you?"

"When I was diagnosed," she said, "I decided I was going to fight it with everything I had. I was going to take control of this and go full blast to beat it."

She reported that she went three times a year to M. D. Anderson, the famous cancer center in Houston. In between visits, she was treated by Louisville doctors. The M. D. Anderson physicians recommended chemotherapy, but the Louisville specialists urged an experimental treatment. This conflict wore her down. "I feel like I'm batting myself back and forth," she said. The disagreement persisted until her death.

Every time she visited Houston, her three sisters accompanied her. In my experience, that was very unusual. They became her support system. She told me that one sister was a critical care nurse, and she was particularly helpful. For another sister, who was the least emotionally stable, these visits to Texas were very difficult, but she made them as a commitment to her sister.

---

1. Thomas Merton, *Thoughts in Solitude* (New York: Farrar, Straus & Giroux, 1999) 79.

Out of those visits to M. D. Anderson came Sarah's mission. She became a messenger to the Louisville medical community, educating people about pancreatic cancer. Her remarkable longevity in the face of this fatal disease encouraged her to distribute information about pancreatic cancer. She found a clearinghouse in Colorado for up-to-date information and discovered that she could be a resource person for doctors and people suffering from pancreatic cancer. She declared, "I want them to know that this isn't a death sentence. The path is different for everyone."

For the last two years of her life, she carried the latest research from M. D. Anderson back to Louisville and presented it to doctors specializing in pancreatic cancer. She reported that some of the Louisville physicians were simply "out of the loop." Some welcomed the information. Others resisted and were insulted. And whenever the advice from Louisville doctors conflicted with the judgments of the Houston specialists, she always sided with the oncologists at M. D. Anderson.

Sarah's mission and message gave new meaning to her life. One of her Houston doctors told Sarah that her desire to live with this specific purpose of bringing news and hope to victims of pancreatic cancer had increased her longevity.

In reporting this amazing and inspiring story, Sarah said nothing about God. She only spoke of her work as a "missionary for information." We continued to meet every two weeks after the retreat. She was very guarded about her relationship with God. It was difficult to understand what my role was for her. I trusted that God would reveal to me what I needed to know and when. I kept praying over that exchange at the retreat, thinking about her latching on to the words of John XXIII about the difficulty of receiving love in our spiritual life.

A month after the retreat—around Thanksgiving—Sarah went to Houston. Her condition had taken a nosedive; the tests showed that the cancer was growing rapidly. While the Louisville doctors continued to advocate an experimental therapy, the Houston doctors told her, "Why do that? You may get a placebo. You'll be wasting your time." They suggested palliative care and hospice, which she rejected out of hand.

Just after Christmas, she went into the hospital in horrendous shape. She had not eaten in a week, and she had a serious blockage between her stomach and intestine. Her stomach had to be pumped, and what emerged was a smelly dark brown and grey substance. She stayed in the hospital for a week. The staff told me they didn't know how she survived, but she did.

She stayed home for a couple of weeks and then returned to Houston. She said she wanted to thank them for their help and say goodbye. When she returned to Louisville, she reentered the hospital but eventually went home.

After leaving the hospital, she visited me twice more at my office. She was always on time, her hands in heavy wool gloves because severe neuropathy made her hands ice cold. She knew the end was near, and she told me, "I want to go to confession." So I led her in what the Catholic Church calls the Sacrament of Reconciliation.

I am bound to confidentiality by the seal of the sacrament, so I cannot describe the details of her confession. But after I read Scripture and allowed time for silent prayer, she spoke. She confessed her sins, expressing regret and sorrow for her actions and omissions. It was a spiritual inventory of shame and humility before God. Later, after we celebrated this sacrament of healing, she said, "I've never voiced this before, but I needed to put it out there before God."

Her life was filled with regret, remorse, and shame and a deep desire for healing and forgiveness from God. She had lived her life as a strong woman—very much in control. Now she was humbled. She knew she was coming to the end of her life, and she said, "I can't meet God with a straight face. I have to say these things."

We had only one more meeting. It was very brief. She was declining rapidly and looked like a shell of herself. Although we were scheduled to meet again the week before Holy Week, she cancelled at the last minute and said she would call after Easter. She never called. She died on Good Friday. Her primary caregiver told me she simply stopped breathing and slipped away.

I couldn't help thinking that this peaceful death was a gift of her coming to some kind of resolution about her entrusting herself to God and falling into the peace of God. All her life had been a struggle—to succeed in business, to deal with herself and others, to fight her disease, and especially to know God. She was one of the most honest people I have ever known. But when she asked God to forgive her during her confession, I felt she was already making the transition to finding God and God's love.

Sarah was one of those people who really questioned what love was all about. She could not understand unconditional love. "That's not the way it works," she told me. "When I cared for my mother, I did it because I had to. I always had my problems with Mother, but when she got sick, I had to take care of her. It was my duty and responsibility. It wasn't love." She had trouble understanding that God could love her, or that she could deserve God, or that she could love herself.

And yet, she searched for God. She repeatedly returned to the words of John XXIII about receiving love, and she said she did not know how to do that. She said she could understand a just God—one who demanded something in exchange for love. But she couldn't understand that God could love her without any expectations. Sarah was one of those people who hear "I love you" and receive it intellectually and believe it, but who can never accept it.

At her final confession, I know that she fell completely into the hands of God. She tasted the love of God that she had been questioning all her life. She had been a skeptic—about God, other people, and herself. But at the end, she trusted God's love for her.

Sarah is like so many people who live at the fringes of the church, and one of the graces of our retreats is that we attract so many like her. The Sarahs of the world are very good for me. They have no patience with the traditional pieties of the church or the spiritual bouquets we sometimes try to offer that don't mean a thing. Her honesty kept me honest. Part of what I believe I can offer the skeptics, the people on the edges, is a nonjudgmental spirit so they can lower their guard.

With Sarah, grace finally broke through skepticism. I don't know how it happened. I trust God to transform people, but I don't understand this mystery. I also know that it's not enough to listen. I have some pretty good listening skills, but I am convinced that what really matters is when I pray for them, intercede with God for them. I am a kind of advance guard, asking for God's presence in their lives. I did that every day for Sarah.

Sarah shared the same spirit with her namesake in Scripture. The biblical Sarah laughed when messengers from God told her she would be blessed with a child. That ancient woman's skepticism about God's gift of love was like the modern Sarah's disbelief. Both Sarahs struck out on a journey—one from Ur to Canaan, the other through the business world of twentieth-century America. As they journeyed, they struggled. And they prayed.

Though we don't know what unfolds after our dying, we trust the God who brings all things to completion. I have faith that both the biblical Sarah and this modern Sarah died with the assurance that God loved them and welcomed them home.

The modern Sarah lived like so many who find themselves doubting God's love, the grace and forgiveness offered in Jesus Christ. They are spiritual skeptics. They simply aren't sure. But I think the Sarah I knew died with the assurance of Thomas Merton's prayer: "Therefore will I trust you always though I may seem to be lost in the shadow of death. I will not fear, for you are ever with me, and you will never leave me to face my perils alone."

Sarah did not die alone. She had found God.

Reflection

Sarah, the self-described "missionary for information," engaged her disease with a "business plan" that would be the envy of any entrepreneur. She was a very accomplished person who controlled her destiny until pancreatic cancer intervened. In her spiritual journey, control became less useful, and honesty grew. God remained an enigma for her—a hope, a dream, and ultimately a mystery of love. She let go of her need to understand God. She prayed Thomas Merton's prayer as her own and found God waiting eagerly for her.

Prayer

Lord, release us from the illusion that our knowledge of you brings us comfort and security. Let us humbly admit that our words and images of you are limited. Instead, give us comfort in knowing that honesty and truthfulness, questions rather than answers, are the pathways to eternal life. Welcome us home, free of the burden of our skepticism, into the bright light of your company forever. Amen.

JACK

The Sad Man Who Told Funny Stories

JACK WAS A BORN storyteller. He could move people to deep laughter, and at one point in his life he'd had a clown ministry, entertaining both children and adults. He had a big, round face and a beautiful smile. He had moved to Louisville from the East, as had I, and our common roots gave us a natural connection. He taught English in one of the Catholic high schools in Louisville, and he loved literature, especially drama.

I met him through a nurse who had assisted us on the Gennesaret Retreats, although it turned out that Jack and I had many overlapping friendships. When I met him, he was in his late fifties and had been diagnosed with brain cancer about six months earlier. My nurse friend said that Jack liked to regale her with his stories. Even his dog, she said, would sit in rapt attention as Jack spun his tales. She became one of his regular visitors, and during one visit she told him about me and the retreat and asked if he would be open to seeing a priest. He said he was, and she passed this word to me.

When I visited Jack, he had already undergone the initial stages of chemotherapy. I saw him at his home, a small bungalow with modest furnishings. It became obvious immediately that Jack had a favorite place—an overstuffed easy chair, directly opposite the door. He offered me tea, and even though I am not a tea drinker I accepted. At first, our conversation was very stilted, and he carefully avoided any talk about his illness. When I asked him directly about his cancer, he began by saying, "I'm not dealing with this well."

Then he was silent. He didn't tell any stories, which I thought was odd since my nurse friend emphasized how much he enjoyed entertaining people with his sagas. Eventually he began to speak—haltingly—about his illness.

"You see this baseball cap?" he said. Taking off the hat and revealing a nearly bald head, he declared, "I used to have dark, wavy hair. This is what it's done to me so far." Tears welled up in his eyes, and he began to take deep swallows. Then followed a long period of silence. Finally, he sighed, "I just have to live with this."

Jack abruptly changed the subject, and we talked about our growing up in the East, travel and some of our favorite trips, and his love of literature, especially English literature. "I love to see students get excited about literature!" he exclaimed, and the more we talked about literature and his teaching, the more gregarious he became. Suddenly he stopped. "But that's all over now."

"That must be really hard on you. And your relationship with God," I said.

Jack responded by telling me about his membership in Louisville's Cathedral of the Assumption. Led by Father Ron Knott, the congregation had dramatically expanded from a handful of elderly women to thousands of parishioners, ranging from the homeless to the wealthy. "I find peace in the diversity of people who worship there," he said. "They come from all over!"

But then Jack turned the topic back to himself. "I wonder if I have enough strength, if I can find peace. I wonder whether God will be with me when I really need it. I guess I have to rely on myself until I get bad."

I have learned that dying people, especially men, want to maintain some kind of control over their lives, at least on the outside. Jack was typical in that regard, but after our meeting, I realized that since he had avoided telling stories, the veneer of control was cracking.

I saw Jack about a month later when I did a spiritual assessment of his suitability for going on the retreat. "Tell me how you find God in your experience now," I suggested.

"Well," he said, "most people talk about how prayer helps them, but that's not me. I find God in everything around me. Other people—that's how I discover God. I see God's wisdom in each one of them."

As Jack described his faith, I became fascinated. He had a very incarnational understanding of the presence of God. When he talked about finding God in other people, he spoke with a deep sense of wonder and mystery. He was awed by God's power. He was deeply thankful for his friends who visited him, but added reluctantly, "Maybe there are others who need attention more than I do. Maybe my friends should be visiting them."

I did not know where this was going, so I remained silent. Jack gradually began talking about people with whom he no longer had contact, including his estranged brother. Although he never explained why he and his brother were estranged, it clearly troubled him. "I have really struggled with how God could be present in our estrangement," he said. "I just don't get it. Or let me give you another example—the homeless people at the cathedral. How is God present for them? I notice them, but a lot of people don't. This is very confusing to me."

"I'll give you another example," Jack continued, his voice rising. "These doctors who see me—I have a lot of anger toward them. They treat conditions, not people. They don't have any awareness of God. God isn't part of their lives."

Jack was clearly agonizing about his relationship with God. "I want to hear God speak," he declared. Pointing to his hearing aids, he added wistfully, "I guess these thing aren't working very well. I don't hear God."

I told him that on the retreat, there would be many opportunities for him to hear God—to be alone and be silent. I asked him how he felt about that, and he said, "Yeah, I'm into that. I'm ready."

Just before the retreat, Jack became seriously ill. Despite his condition, he postponed a chemotherapy treatment to go on the retreat. When he arrived, he immediately reverted to form. He began telling one story after another and became the center of everyone's attention. They laughed at his jokes, including the ones in which he poked fun at himself and his hair loss. He was a one-man show, and the other retreatants loved him.

During a break, Jack sidled up to me. "Where am I going to find God in all this?" he asked.

I had begun to tire of his playing games. I wondered whether he was willing to ask some hard questions of himself and God. I responded rather curtly, "You're in a monastery—a place where people encounter God," I told him. "God is all around you. I'm not sure you've really entered this space. You are physically here, but you seem lost." Jack became very quiet and turned away.

After the break, I made a presentation on the meaning of the cross and presented small crosses to each of the participants to hang around their necks. "This cross symbolizes God and the vertical connection we have with him and the horizontal connection we have with others," I told them. "You need to claim that victory which is yours through Christ." I watched Jack especially as he slowly put the crucifix around his neck.

Afterward I found him slowly walking around the circular drive in front of the monastery. I started walking with him but said nothing. In the middle of the circle was a statue of St. Joseph. After several passes around the drive, Jack stopped and pointed at the statue. "I wonder if I will ever be that high," he said. "I wonder if I will ever be like that."

"What's preventing you?" I asked.

"My unforgiveness of my brother," Jack said. Then he clammed up and said nothing more about this during the rest of the retreat.

Jack had some very close friends who helped take care of him, and three of these men picked him up after the retreat. A few weeks later he was back in the hospital, and one of his friends told me that Jack wanted to see me.

He was a mess. He looked horrible. "I want to talk about my brother," he announced, and then the real story within Jack came out. I learned that his brother was dead, which came as a big surprise to me because I had assumed he was still living.

"My brother and I took care of our father as he died," Jack said. "We were the primary caregivers. But we argued about it. They were real knock-down, drag-out fights. Finally, I told him, 'Okay, he's yours. You take care of him!'"

After his father's death, Jack moved from the East to Louisville. There was no communication with his brother, and this went on for years. As he described his brother, Jack's anger and resentment welled up within him. "There was no partnership with him," he emphasized. "He was so domineering. After we separated, I tried to reconnect, but he shunned me. I called but he wouldn't answer. Finally, he sent me one letter. In it he said, 'You are no longer in my life.'"

Jack continued, "You remember that statue at the monastery? That statue is what I've been searching for. My brother was named Joseph. That statue—that peace—is what I am seeking."

Jack's pain cut me deeply. Here was a man dying of cancer and yet holding on to an unresolved break with his brother, who had already died. I wondered if he could be at peace while still holding on to that resentment.

About five days before he died, I received word that Jack wanted to see me again. We didn't talk long, and before I left I prayed that God would relieve him of his resentment and that his anger would be transformed into grace. When I said, "Amen," I looked at Jack, and on his big, round face I saw the trace of a smile.

Jack was one of those people who showed one face to others while underneath was a different person. His stories covered up the story of his soul. His humor disguised the pain in his heart. One of the last things he gave me was a goofy little hat with an attached hairpiece. Jack wanted to go out as a funny man who told stories and made people laugh, perhaps because he knew so much sadness inside.

Later his friends told me how much the retreat had meant to him. They said he found that God could be present with him as he was. At the last, Jack became confident that he could meet God. This isn't to say that Jack's issues with his brother disappeared. Not everything was resolved for him when he died. He was a teacher trying to learn more.

I knew Jack for less than a year, but I was deeply touched by his heartfelt desire to be restored to his brother. One time he quoted back to me my words about the victory of God in the cross of Christ that connects us to God and to others. Jack reminded me that people have to be reconciled with others in order to be reconciled with God. The unresolved relationships of our lives have to be settled before we meet God face to face, and Jack the teacher taught me that lesson in the way he died.

Reflection

Jack's journey was a precious blend of pathos and humor. Storytellers are lost without an audience eager to listen. Jack never lacked an audience seeking his humor; people were eager to hear him. But pathos required a more intimate listening heart, a face-to-face personal contact that only a friend could offer. Luckily, Jack had both. Even more importantly, he knew he had God's listening heart. Humor may serve as a path of denial for some as they die; for Jack it was an act of faith and courage.

Prayer

Spirit of the living God, revive us. In the midst of our pain and suffering fill us with a spirit of humor. Let us discover the redeeming power of laughter and the comfort of a loving smile given and received. Keep us hopeful, alive with a spirit of humor and storytelling, so that we might have light in darkness and eternal life in our dying. Amen.

JUDY

The Woman Who Could Not Forgive Herself

I MET JUDY BECAUSE two people called me about her. One was a lay Catholic hospital visitor and the other a student chaplain. I was told there was a woman who wanted to see a priest—"someone I can talk to," as Judy put it. They disclosed virtually nothing about her and why she wanted to talk to a priest except to say that she had inoperable cancer and four months to live. The chaplain told me, "This is a hurting person who has a long history of wounds."

Judy was in her late thirties when I got to know her. She was not physically attractive, her slender body having been decimated by her disease. She wore no jewelry. She was about 5' 7" with reddish brown hair with streaks in it, and she had bushy eyebrows and dark eyes. Her voice had a strong nasal quality. To be honest, I found it annoying.

When I entered her hospital room, I greeted her by her first name as I always do. I was struck first by her eyes. They were filled with fear. It was a hauntingly eerie look, one of deep sadness and fear, but in retrospect, most of what I saw there was simply fear.

Because of what I had been told about her, I decided my role would be one of listening. Judy immediately asked whether our conversation would be confidential. I assured her it would be. With that, she began to tell me about her life. I have discovered in my ministry with dying people that they frequently want to tell their life story because they haven't found someone who will listen. I believe these are sacred stories; my listening honors each person's experience. In telling their story, they are implicitly saying, "This is important. I'm important." With Judy, I resolved that I would button my lips, be as comfortable as I could be, and simply listen.

Surprisingly, Judy leaped into her story at the deep end. "I have a great fear of dying because of my loose living," she said. She never used the word *immoral*, but that is what she meant. "When I was about eighteen," she continued, "I got into heavy drug use. It was mainly LSD but also some other drugs, and I was very promiscuous. I'm afraid I may have picked up AIDS."

I asked, "Have you ever said that to anyone? I mean, have you talked to a doctor?"

"No," she said. "I might have mentioned some of my symptoms, but I never went into any details. I wonder whether AIDS is part of my illness. I'm frightened that I may have infected someone else." As Judy talked, I was struck by the fact that she focused on AIDS, not her cancer.

Judy told me that her heavy drug use and promiscuity took place before she married in her early twenties. She went into some detail about her lifestyle, and I began wondering, "Why is she telling me this? Is this a confession of some sort? Is she asking for forgiveness?" It was very intense and confusing to me.

Judy said she was helped by a group that wanted to bring her out of her drug use and promiscuity. Her future husband was part of the group. "His motives were not for me," she said bitterly. "He was into some very strange sexual behavior. He described our marriage as 'an open marriage,' and I felt like a piece of property. We had multiple partners at his insistence, and one time, he pressured me into bestiality. We eventually split after two years."

After her divorce, Judy tried to find a job without any employment history. She got a position with a kind of mom-and-pop company where she had some secretarial and bookkeeping responsibilities. She committed what she called "petty larceny," and her boss discovered it. He immediately fired her but was good enough not to turn her in to the police.

"So here I am," she said. "I've got a death sentence from my doctor. I have four months to live. I need to talk to you. I need forgiveness because I feel so guilty."

At this point, she had been talking to me for about an hour and a half, and this, again, was only our first meeting. I was overwhelmed. It was so intense, and I had a rising sense of fear. The more she talked, the more she frightened me. What she disclosed to me was simply bizarre. I decided I would be as kind as I could be but wanted to get out of there quickly. I found myself praying that I wouldn't run away from her.

Suddenly she stopped talking, and silence filled the room. When she started up again, she asked for the Sacrament of Reconciliation (confession) and the Anointing of the Sick. In my experience, it's rare for dying people to ask for the Sacrament of Reconciliation, but her request was exactly what she wanted and needed.

"What is your greatest need?" I asked.

"It's my sinful ways," Judy replied. "I'm afraid God will not be willing to forgive me." Note that she said God would not be "willing," not that God would not be able to forgive her.

"How did you come to that conclusion?" I asked.

"Look at what I've told you," she responded vigorously. "Nobody could forgive all that!" Her heart was crying out for some kind of assurance that reconciliation wasn't a theoretical possibility but something she could know without divine judgment.

"The Sacrament of Reconciliation," I said, "is a ritual to show God's love and mercy for you. It's real, and it's for you."

Our conversation had now been going on for more than two hours, with the usual hospital interruptions to take her temperature and adjust her IVs. Finally I asked her if she had other concerns.

"I'm wondering what would be a fitting end to my life," she declared. That dramatically raised my antennae. I immediately became worried that she might be talking about taking her own life by overdosing on her medications.

Judy continued, "Not very many people even know me. Maybe I should just die and no one will know about it. I'll just go away."

I asked, "Is there anybody who knows your story? Do you have any family members?"

She explained that her father had died when she was very young. Her mother stepped out of her life when Judy was on drugs. She was an only child. "I don't have anyone," she flatly declared. "There's no one who knows my story."

I couldn't believe that, but I decided this wasn't the time for any kind of therapy. Here was a woman who was seemingly and utterly alone. So I said, "I will make a promise to you. I will walk with you through this experience of dying. I will walk with you as a friend in Christ, but you're free to tell me to take a walk. And I'll bury you in whatever way is a comfort to you now." She began to cry, and so did I.

I told her I would come back the next day. After three exhausting hours, I needed some time to sort this out.

The following day I visited Judy again. I asked her what she needed to tell me. She immediately clammed up.

"I said too much yesterday," she said. "You're a stranger. I don't know who the hell you are. I don't know what got into me."

I responded, "You called for someone who would listen to you, and that's what you got. You needed to tell me a story, and that's what you gave me."

At this, she relaxed a little and launched into what would be a recurring theme in our talks. "I'm embarrassed by all this. It's not a pretty story. I'm not sure what you think of me. I'm worried that you will find my story repulsive and walk out and never connect with me again. Will you stick with me?"

After pausing for a moment, I said, "I promised to walk with you and bury you in whatever way you desire."

Sometimes, when people have deep regrets about their past, I use the term *toxic* to describe their memories. I told Judy, "I think your story is toxic to you. The details don't bother me, but you seem to be killing yourself—not physically but spiritually and emotionally."

There was a long silence. She never directly responded to that. When Judy finally spoke, she said, "So you'll still listen and be with me?"

"Yes, in whatever way you want me to be."

As I left, I told her I would call the next morning if I couldn't make it back to the hospital. When I called, I learned that she was getting ready to be discharged and arrangements were being made for palliative care through hospice.

The next time I saw Judy, it was at her home. It was a very simple apartment and sparsely furnished. She had very few possessions, and what struck me was that there were no pictures of anything or anybody. Her dining table was covered with medical supplies; there were no letters, no newspapers, no mail of any sort. There was nothing personal—nothing that would indicate she lived there. Her apartment reminded me that she really was alone—no family, no friends. It frightened me. I thought, "This is all going to fall on my shoulders." In some ways that's exactly what happened.

Judy told me she was overwhelmed by the care she was receiving from hospice, especially one nurse who was very kind to her and listened to her. But, as is so common among dying people, she cycled back again to our first conversation. She was desperate. "I'm not worthy!" she cried. "God will never forgive me. I'm going straight to hell!"

I spent that visit reassuring her that forgiveness is a process. I told her there is a ritual for forgiveness—the Sacrament of Reconciliation—but at a deep level, it was a process that takes time. "The challenge," I said, "is to accept what God is already offering you. God wants you to accept forgiveness. God wants you to accept his love and mercy."

At that, she was very quiet.

In my subsequent visits, Judy would return to the subject of her shame and guilt. But in one conversation, I could see a shift. "I remember," Judy told me, "that you said I have to forgive myself."

I asked her, "Do you know the Our Father?"

"Of course," she replied. "I say it every day."

I said, "In that prayer, we ask that God will forgive us even as we forgive others. The other is you. When you hold on to your sin, it is a barrier that inhibits you from receiving forgiveness." And then I asked her a very hard question: "Can you forgive yourself?"

I remember her eyes softening. Where before I had seen fear, suddenly there was light. Her eyes even opened wider. As the old saying goes, "The eyes are the windows of the soul," and I could see that something was happening in Judy.

On my next visit, I saw that her eyes were open much wider than before. They weren't as bloodshot, and the worn, tired look had softened a lot. Her eyes filled her face more graciously. I told her, "You look different to me. What's changed?"

"You noticed?"

"Yes, I noticed something."

"It's my eyes and my face," Judy said, "When I first saw you, my eyes were filled with fear. I just knew you would judge me. Now I feel different. The one hospice nurse who is so kind—she listens to me without judgment, just like you."

It became clear to me that Judy's healing was happening through herself, to herself, as she looked at herself with different eyes. She wasn't quite at the point of forgiving herself, but her wall of guilt was cracking. Her eyes and face had softened. Even her voice was different; it was gentle.

After about three months, I asked her again about her plans for her funeral. "I've made some decisions," she announced. I didn't respond, and there was silence. "I don't want a funeral or a funeral Mass. But I would like to be cremated and buried in a Catholic cemetery. I doubt anyone will come. It's my passage. It's my dying." And then, in a stunning insight, she declared, "But I want to respect my body even though it's been a source of sin for me because I know it's loved and forgiven by God."

Judy was a different person than the one I had met a few short months ago. She had begun to forgive herself to some degree. She showed this in how she wanted her body handled after her death. There would be no grieving, only a simple prayer service, but she wanted her ashes buried.

The last time I visited Judy was in the hospice unit of the hospital. She couldn't eat and had very little strength. I gave her a crucifix with a cord, and I wrapped the cord around her hand. I said a prayer, and after it Judy moved her lips. I couldn't hear her, so I bent over and put my ear near her mouth. She whispered, "Thank you."

She died the next morning. Hospice and the hospital referred everything to me. She had actually selected a funeral home and a cemetery, but when the funeral director asked me to write her obituary, I told him I simply didn't know enough about her. Two days after she died, we took her ashes to the cemetery. The funeral director was also a Catholic, and I said to him, "The most meaningful prayer for her was the Our Father. She learned what it meant to her very personally. Let's commit her soul to God who is merciful. Let's be assured that the peace of God has now overwhelmed all of her guilt and all of her confusion and doubt and despair. Let's pray the Our Father."

And that's what we did.

Only the funeral director, a couple of employees of the cemetery, and I were there. Judy rested in peace.

Reflection

The single most damaging effect of any serious sinful act is the conviction that God will not forgive us. Judy was convinced this was true. There was no doubt in her mind that God would turn away from her. Her sins were too great and toxic even to God. She wrapped herself in shame, profound regret, and hopelessness until Abba set her free. As she prayed the Our Father, God's mercy freed her. She received a mantel of grace and love from God that set her free.

Prayer

Abba, we hunger for your forgiveness and love; we yearn for freedom from our guilt and sinful behavior. Grant us your mercy; fill us with your compassionate love; open our hearts to your forgiveness, and give us a new vision to see ourselves as you see us. We thank you for your willingness and desire to set us free. Amen.

NICK

The Man Who Lived in a Crate

I MET NICK WHEN I was serving a large suburban congregation in New Jersey. His wife was Nikki. That's right—Nick and Nikki. Their names were the source of great amusement in our parish.

Nikki was the active parishioner. I saw Nick at high points in the year, such as Christmas and Easter, but that was about it. He was a hidden figure—very introverted—and nearly always stayed at home. Unlike Nikki, who was very talkative and vivacious, Nick didn't socialize easily. I came to discover that this was the way he lived most of his life.

Nick was a tall, lanky guy—probably about 6′2″, with a full head of hair. He was an accountant and wore black, heavy-rimmed glasses. I hate to say this, but he was one of those men who doesn't wear a suit quite right. He was always polite, but whenever I saw him, I got the idea that he was saying, "I don't care how I look. Let's get the job done."

Nikki was his polar opposite. While Nick was tall and quiet, she was short and always had something to say. Even though Nick looked rather unkempt, Nikki dressed very neatly. She had long, curly hair, and smiles came easily to her face. She was a great storyteller. People liked her and she made them feel comfortable. She was a housewife with many friends who loved her sense of humor.

Nick was diagnosed with cancer after routine blood work for a physical exam. He was only in his late fifties. It was a complete surprise. One Sunday after Mass, Nikki told me about his cancer and said, "I don't know how he's going to handle this. Right now we're going to Sloan-Kettering. We'll know more in a week or so."

They discovered that he had stage three liver cancer. I suspected that this might be due to alcoholism, but I didn't inquire about that and Nikki never volunteered any information. I wondered how this accountant, who spent his life focusing on details and who left socializing to his wife, would handle such a grave diagnosis. I asked Nikki, "How is he handling this?"

With an uncharacteristic pinched face, Nikki said, "He's closed up completely. He's shut down. He won't talk at all. He refers to his cancer as 'it.' Do you think you can visit?"

"I can visit," I said, "but does he want a visit?"

"I'm not sure," Nikki said, "but would you at least try?"

"You set a time," I responded, "and we'll see if we can talk." She told me she would try to arrange it, but it would have to be late morning. He simply didn't move much early in the day, and he took naps in the afternoon.

She told me that Nick was cutting off all contact with everyone, including her and his two grown sons. He was isolating himself more than he ever did before. His accounting work for individuals and small companies had given him the option of working from home, and now he barricaded himself there. He had always been a recluse, but now he was practically a hermit. Later she described him as a man who had lost all hope and was in total despair.

I quickly realized two things. One, in a sense I would be meeting a total stranger, and two, in another sense I would be meeting someone who was totally alienated from himself and his condition.

When I arrived for my first meeting with Nick, I entered a small ranch-style house. From the living room, there was a hallway to the master bedroom—Nick's sacred space. He was sitting in a chair looking out the window and facing away from the door. When Nikki announced, "Father Paul is here," he never moved an inch, not even his head.

I immediately sensed his resistance. I felt as if I was intruding in his space. Nikki and I approached him. She stood in front of him, and I stood at his side. I put my hand on his shoulder. As I normally do when I touch people, I did it very gently, and I kept my hand there. I could feel the tension running across his shoulders. He was very rigid. It was like touching steel.

"Nick," I said, "I'm here to see how you're doing."

He shrugged his shoulders and didn't say anything.

I thought to myself: this is going nowhere fast. It hit me that Nick was living in a box. Actually, it was more like a crate, and he had hammered the boards together from the inside. And I didn't know what was in it.

I fumbled for an opening. "It must be terrible to get this news—so unexpected," I said. "What was it like to hear about your cancer?"

"Nothing I could do about it," he mumbled.

"How did you feel?"

"I don't know what I felt."

"Nick," I asked, "do you pray?"

"No."

"What would be helpful to you?"

"To be left alone."

"Would you like me to pray?"

"If you want to."

So, I offered a simple prayer for God's blessing for Nick and made the sign of the cross on his forehead, laying hands on him in silence before I left the room. I was quietly asking God to give strength to him and wisdom to me.

When we got outside the bedroom, I told Nikki, "I don't know what will be helpful. His resistance is so great." She agreed. "Let me suggest," I said, "that we try regular visits two or three times a month. I'll just stop by to see how he's doing. And I will pray for him."

She replied, "I think that's about the only thing you can do. Nick's getting more and more hopeless and depressed." She shook her head. "He's a stranger to us now. This is so unlike him. He's so withdrawn and not engaged. Even though he's stiff in public, in our family he's always been warm and supportive. He's been a kind and gentle man with his family, but not anymore."

In some ways, this didn't surprise me. When disease strikes quickly, it shatters an individual's securities. The routine of life is broken completely.

As time went on and as I visited regularly, I wondered if Nick felt any passion or anger against God, but he never expressed it. He suffered from depression more than outrage. Gingerly I began to ask open-ended but searching questions about God and his family, and he slowly emerged from his crate. As I posed these questions, I could see that Nick was starting to think about his answers. We danced around each other, with Nick struggling to express his thoughts and feelings and me trying to explore them.

One time I asked him, "What do you think is the purpose in all of this?"

He responded, "If there is one, it's not good."

"What does that mean?"

"Because I will die. Because everything I've lived for will be gone. Everything will be wasted."

"What do you think will endure beyond your death?"

"Well, I guess my family will remember me."

"How?"

"You know, they'll gather around and do small talk. Just simple stuff." Then Nick paused and added, "I guess I'm important to them."

In my visits, I tried posing even more open-ended questions about big issues—loss, love, relationships, God. I keenly felt his inability to talk about his feelings; he simply had no affect in his voice, his face, or his body. I often felt we were spinning a spider web, and I couldn't find my way. Nick was one of the most difficult people I have ever encountered in my entire ministry.

I finally realized that I had to learn to surrender my need to get to Nick's heart.

About halfway in my journey with him, he gradually became more comfortable talking with me. He started attending church regularly, but as the cancer grew worse he came only occasionally. At home, he initially refused the Eucharist, which is very unusual for housebound people. But closer to his death, he did accept it—first from his wife and then from lay parish ministers.

The pattern to his illness was the familiar rollercoaster cycle of good times and bad times created by his chemotherapy. I tried to make my visits only on the upside. As he was approaching the end, he began to get more and more engaged.

One time he asked, "I guess God has a purpose? A plan? I guess this is his will for me?" He looked at me intently and posed the question no priest wants to hear: "Is that what you think?"

I swallowed and replied, "I can't answer for God, but I'm conscious by being with you that asking that question means you realize God is with you in this. God's not separate from you."

I really wanted to affirm that. I couldn't answer his question rationally. It's unanswerable. But even though there's no answer, only a person of faith can ask the question, and I had to encourage Nick to see that. God did care for him. He needed to hear and feel God's love.

Closer to his death, I witnessed something I have seen many times. Nick pulled his wife and two sons to him—each one privately—and he said goodbye. These intimate times are very important—to the dying and to those they love.

Nick eventually returned to what he had been before. He left his crate. He turned his back on his isolation and reconnected. It was very dramatic and had a huge impact on his family. He also began to speak to me with a passion about God that I had not heard before. He wanted to know God rather than what God is doing.

"When I get to meet God," he said, "I've got a lot of questions."

"Like what?" I asked.

"Well, of course I want to know why this would happen. But I also want to know why I came into the world in the first place. What does my life mean?"

He started to live with a heartfelt connection to God—not God in the abstract, but how God related to him. The accountant who was good with details was gradually grasping how things were coming together for him. As Nikki told me, "His best self is coming out."

He began to focus more of his attention on what I would describe as "dying well." He became more engaged with what was happening, and I could see a sense of peace coming over him. This wasn't what some people call "acceptance." It was peacefulness. He showed me how he was living through this with God.

Nick was transformed in the brief nine months I knew him. His isolation was very strong, but he knocked down the planks of his crate and climbed out. His journey to dying was a time to engage and wonder what was unfolding.

God uses time like that. Nick finally resisted the idea that his disease was something being done to him and moved to the point of engagement with God in a way he had never experienced before.

As Nick approached his death, he found a vocabulary to speak about his relationship with God and God's presence with him. Nick the accountant, a man who had tracked transactions all his life, opened up and found a relationship with God.

Reflection

In critical illness, isolation can be self-imposed. Nick closed himself off to his family, those nearest to him, his professional colleagues, and God. He did not talk about his feelings; he discovered very little about what he was dealing with. This isolation disarms caregivers. It torments loved ones who cannot touch the person they love. In this situation God waits patiently, giving time for love to seep through to someone like Nick. Private conversations, heart-to-heart talks with his sons and wife, opened the passage for love to enter his life. God speaks through others; God listens and comforts and waits patiently for us to come home forever.

Prayer

Lord, the shock and confusion of our illness and dying overwhelm us. Empower us to speak heart to heart to our loved ones; give us courage and hope that they will understand our struggle. We know that you are present, patiently loving us in our distress. May our family and friends listen with your heart and give us your undivided attention. Amen.

MARY

The Woman Who Knew God in Silence and Peace

MARY SUFFERED FROM ALS—LOU Gehrig's disease. She was a very slight woman, only about 5' 2" tall, and she weighed no more than one hundred pounds. When I got to know her, she had just celebrated her sixty-fourth birthday and was still ambulatory. She carried herself with great dignity, and in her bearing, you knew she was comfortable with herself. She was married and had three children (two daughters and one son) and seven grandchildren.

Meeting Mary was something of a fluke. I was substituting for a pastor and covering Mass for him. I had to ad lib the homily since I had no time to prepare notes or a written sermon, and I noticed that Mary was very attentive as I spoke. After Mass, she told me, "I've heard a lot about you and your ministry in pastoral care."

"Are you a caregiver?" I asked.

"No, I'm receiving care," she said.

"I hope it's helpful."

"What I'm confronting needs all my attention."

I encouraged her to call me. I didn't hear anything for about a month, and then Mary contacted me and mentioned the Gennesaret Retreats. I set up a time to visit her at home and to listen to her story. Mary began by saying she had been diagnosed with ALS a year earlier. Before that she had experienced difficulty holding objects and had problems with her speech. At first, the doctors thought she might have suffered transient strokes (TIAs) but then settled on ALS as the cause of her problems. "It was like being thrown against a brick wall," she said. "It hit me: Who is going to pick up the pieces?"

She explained that at first she refused to accept the diagnosis, and she was convinced they had made a mistake. She sought a second opinion from a regional medical center for ALS, where the diagnosis was confirmed. All of her subsequent treatment came at this center.

"I was told there was no cure," she said. "All they could do was to slow the progression of the disease. They gave me no time line, but we learned via the Internet that it was likely to be about eighteen to twenty-four months. So, maybe I should go on that retreat."

I asked her, "Where is God with you? Are you angry? Resentful?"

"I'm not angry," she replied. "Just numb. I'm still in a state of shock. I have so much to live for." She then talked about her husband, children, and grandchildren. "I'm very involved in caring for them," she said.

"Where's God in that?" I asked.

Mary replied, "I listened to you at Mass. You said God always gives us strength to bear anything that comes our way."

"Do you believe that?"

"I believe it with my mind but not with my spirit."

"Would you like to bring that on the retreat?"

"Well, maybe there are others who are sicker than me who should go."

Mary said she would talk to her husband, and two weeks later she called me to say she wanted to go on the retreat. The retreat nurse coordinator visited her and did a full medical history and evaluation. Afterward, she called and told me that Mary had a very deep spiritual life. "She knows God," she reported, "but she is searching for more and wants to go deeper."

I followed up with a spiritual assessment of her suitability for the retreat. Mary's evaluation was one of the most articulate spiritual assessments I have ever done. When I asked her how she was handling her disease and how her family was handling her disease, she talked mainly about her family. She was very anxious about how they would care for themselves while caring for her, and her concern was especially directed toward her husband. I probed her on how the retreat might help her with her worry. "How will you know God is helping you on the retreat and speaking to you?" I asked.

She replied simply, "Silence and a deep sense of peace."

While I was there, I met her husband, Frank. He was gone a great deal because he was an independent contractor who drove semitrucks. He didn't match the stereotype of a truck driver at all. He was a very gentle soul, very quiet and reflective. He wasn't nearly as articulate about his faith as Mary was, but he did tell me that his mission was to provide as much care to Mary as possible. I asked him whether he wanted to go on the retreat, and he declined, saying, "No, that would distract Mary from her communion with God."

Before the retreat, Mary contracted pneumonia and had to be hospitalized. This was her first significant complication from ALS. I visited her in the hospital, and at the end of our talk, she asked, "Will you pray for me?" I laid my hands on her. I didn't say any words. It just seemed right. It lasted for quite a while, and then I made the sign of the cross. She couldn't talk easily, so it seemed she wanted a different kind of presence.

Mary was released from the hospital, and she had one more treatment at the regional medical center before she went on the retreat.

When I lead these retreats, I am frequently amazed by how God acts through the right person, with the right people, in the right time, in the right way. Before the retreat, Mary was worried that other people would pity her. The staff was concerned that she would be too much of a burden for them. She was only the second ALS patient to go on a retreat, and the first one had proved to be a great challenge to the staff. What happened was that Mary became a deep witness, not to how she was handling her disease, but to her faith. And I later learned what a profound impact she had on the staff themselves. She ministered to them as much as they cared for her. That has never happened to the same extent with anyone else.

During one of my sessions with the retreat participants, I focused on the theme of God's love. I used what is probably my favorite quotation. It comes from Pope John XXIII, who said, "The greatest challenge of the spiritual life is not to love but to receive love." I worked with this theme in various ways, and at the end I walked up to each participant, said his or her name, and declared, "You are loved by God. God says, 'I love you.'" When I said that to Mary, I knew that God had spoken through me to her. I had connected with her.

During the retreat, I could tell that Mary was losing the grip in her hands. She was having difficulty holding on to utensils, and her handshake was very weak. When we celebrated the Adoration of the Blessed Sacrament, Mary indicated that she wanted me to hold the sacrament in my hands at a level close to her face. Since she was seated, I had to kneel before her. This lasted at least ten minutes. My knees were aching, and my legs and arms were shaking. But I sensed that something was going on. She desired, she wanted this time with God.

Mary was a spiritual introvert, I realized. She processed things inside her. Afterward, I didn't push her. The Adoration was her time for silence and peace.

At the end of the retreat, I said goodbye to Mary and said I would be in contact with her. Two weeks later I received a note from her, thanking me for the retreat and telling me that she had shared the retreat with her family. I knew her pastor was very good about visiting her, and I had reports about how her family cared for her, scheduling family gatherings every Sunday. They were tender and gentle with her.

When I visited her, it was clear that the ALS was progressing. Mary told me about her latest visit to the regional medical center. There she had learned how to use a keyboard to communicate, and she showed me how she could do it. She was very playful and funny about it. Suddenly it struck me that when the question of who is the greatest arises with Jesus, he declared it was a child. Here was Mary, acting like a child, full of life and fun. That was a very special experience.

She continued to attend Mass regularly, in her wheelchair, first under her own power and eventually pushed by her husband or a member of the family. Since she could no longer speak, she learned to communicate through little buttons that had images on them. There was some discussion about her going to the hospice unit of a hospital, but Mary rejected that. Hospice did provide care for her at home, and she received medications to relax her so that she could breathe easily. She died at home—very peacefully—surrounded by her family.

One family member told me, "We're glad her suffering is over. We got a great gift from her—the gift of peace."

Mary, who knew God in silence and peace, gave that gift to her family. It reminded me of the words of Jesus in the Gospel of John: "Peace I leave with you; my peace I give to you. I do not give to you as the world gives. Do not let your hearts be troubled, and do not let them be afraid" (14:27). She was a remarkable woman, and her dying was a great loss to her family and friends. But she left a legacy—her knowledge of God in silence and peace.

Her family selected a memory card for her funeral, and on it was a poem that captured much of Mary's life and the way she greeted death:

> When I come to the end of the day
> And the sun has set for me
> I want no rites in a gloom-filled room.
> Why cry for a soul set free?

Miss me a little, but not too long
And not with your head bowed low.
Remember the love we once shared—
Miss me, but let me go.

For this is a journey we all must take
And each must go alone.
It's all a part of the Maker's plan,
A step on the road to home.
When you are lonely and sick at heart
Go to the friends we know
And bury your sorrows
In doing good deeds—
Miss me, but let me go.

Reflection

Struggling with the terminal illness ALS (Lou Gehrig's disease) means a slow and inevitable loss of control that Mary knew would limit her ability to communicate and function. She engaged with her doctors and family as the disease progressed and sought the strength and peace of God in deep, intimate moments of silence. Silence was her inner window to a deep sense of peace. Mary witnessed to the peace of God, not through actions or words, but through the testimony of her living. For others she became the embodiment of the Scripture that says, "for he is not the God of disorder but of peace" (1 Cor 14:33).

Prayer

Lord, hold us firmly secure in your peace, as we struggle with pain and hopelessness. Grant us the wisdom to know you as the abiding center of our life, our strength, and grace. Lead us through the complex path of illness toward you. Let our death be peaceful and secure in your love. Amen.

MILDRED

The Woman Who Sought Peace in a Life of Chaos

I MET MILDRED EARLY in my ministry when I was an associate pastor of a large suburban congregation in New Jersey. She regularly attended daily Mass, which I usually conducted. She was in her late fifties, married, with no children. Rather sickly, she suffered from diabetes and had poor circulation, especially in her feet. Amputation was one of her constant concerns. She had grey curly hair and wore glasses. Among the other parishioners, she stood out because she dressed poorly. Her clothes were always out of date. She came across as someone who always looked sad and was constantly pessimistic.

When it came time in the Mass for daily petitions when people could mention their prayer concerns, Mildred always offered the same two petitions: "Strength and courage for me and others to get through the day, and blessings for all children who have been abandoned." Nobody ever knew to whom she was referring.

She had a rather strange religiosity. In the foyer of the church was a statue of the Sacred Heart of Jesus, and Mildred would talk to it. During Mass when we prayed the Our Father, she would always raise her arms to heaven, way above her head and higher than anyone else's. She always made sure she received Holy Communion last. I would place the host in her hands; she would kiss it three times, and then she would consume the sacred host.

Needless to say, most people thought she was strange. Some regarded her as crazy, perhaps psychotic. Most people avoided her. She was an incredibly hard person to be around with her mumbling, her broad gesturing, and her disheveled appearance.

I tolerated her. I didn't have a clue how to engage her because I never knew what she would do. Given what I later learned, I wish I could say that

I loved her from the start, but I really didn't. I wish I could have related to her in a better way, but I kept my distance.

Then came an incident that changed things.

One day we had to move daily Mass from the chapel to the main church. Only fifteen to twenty people attended daily Mass, so moving from the intimacy of a chapel that seated about thirty-five people to the main church that seated about six hundred was a major shift in the atmosphere of worship. In the chapel, we gathered in a circle around the altar for the liturgy of Eucharist, and everyone received Holy Communion and then returned to their seats. In the main church, however, this small group had to climb four steps in the sanctuary in order to gather in a circle around the altar.

When it came time for communion, I invited everyone to come forward. Mildred stayed seated in her pew. I went down to get her and helped her up the stairs by holding her arm. I wouldn't understand the power of my action until later. She repeated her pattern of receiving Holy Communion last. Others in the daily Mass group helped her back to her seat.

About a month later during my daily visits to a local hospital's intensive care units, I found her in intensive cardiac care. I explained to her that I did not have the Eucharist with me. I said I had only holy oils for the anointing of the sick. When I asked her if I could bring her communion later, she replied, "Yes, I need my communion. I need my communion. I need my communion."

This immediately struck me as very strange. I had never heard anyone refer to the Lord's Supper as "my communion." But I overlooked it as another one of Mildred's eccentricities and asked, "What happened to you? How are you doing now? This must be a rough time for you. Is anyone helping you?"

Mildred replied, "Well, I called my neighbor. She found me on the floor and called an ambulance. That's how I got here. They tell me I had a massive heart attack."

"Where is your husband?" I asked.

"He's not involved. He's not here."

"Shall I call him?"

"No, no, no," she said emphatically. "Don't bother him."

"But you're going to have triple bypass surgery. That's major surgery."

"No, leave him out of this."

I anointed her, and as I was leaving, I thought that there had to be another story going on here. I promised to return later with Holy Communion.

Mildred had her triple bypass surgery, and since this was the early 1980s, when patients were hospitalized far longer than they are today, I knew I would see her several times in the hospital. On my first visit to her in the intensive care unit, I gently said to her, "Mildred, before your operation, you asked me not to contact your husband. Has he come to visit you?"

"No," she said. "I don't expect him to be here."

Here is where I began to get the link between her religious practice and her own life situation. This is what she told me.

"You remember when you helped me up the stairs in the church during daily Mass?" she began. "I was so touched by your kindness that day. I know people always avoid me, especially men."

I said, "You sound like a wounded person. Is there anything you want to tell me?"

"Well," she said in a faint voice, "you were kind to me, so I'm going to trust you now. I've never told anyone this. I was sexually abused by my father when I was a child. I've wondered if I was the cause of that. So I've avoided people, especially men, ever since. I've been haunted by the memory of that abuse."

"You've never told anyone?" I asked.

"No, never."

She said that when I helped her up the stairs, I was the first man to touch her in a nonaggressive way. "You see, I'm married to an abusive alcoholic. He abuses me physically, emotionally, and sexually. He keeps me tied down. He rations out the money to me. I never have enough for food. I never have enough for clothes, so that's why I buy them from the rescue mission. Everything I have has to come from him."

Then she paused for a long time, gathering her strength. "I live in a prison with no escape," she declared. "My communion is my one moment of peace in a life of chaos."

"How can you go home to this?" I asked. "Can I get the hospital social worker to help you?"

"No!" she practically shouted. "That would only make things worse."

Part of me wanted to contact the social worker anyway, but I told her, "We can talk about this again before you leave the hospital."

I checked with the hospital chaplain, who was a friend of mine, and told him what was happening to Mildred. I discovered that she had told him of her husband's cruelty, so the two of us informed the hospital social worker that it was not safe for her to go home. The social worker made a formal report to the state's Department of Youth and Family Services. As a result, Mildred was not sent home but transferred to a cardiac rehab center.

I visited her regularly there and began to learn more about her. During one visit, I said, "Mildred, tell me more about your religious situation. What is this 'my communion' you talk about?"

She told me, "If it's true that God is a God of peace, then communion is my peace. That's all I live for—one moment of peace in a life of chaos. My one moment of peace in a life of chaos." She said it again: "My one moment of peace in a life of chaos." Then she was silent and finally stated, "I doubt I can expect anything more."

As Mildred rested in the rehab center, the state intervened with her husband, and he said he would clean up his act. So, she was discharged to her home.

A month later she showed up at daily Mass, which was now back in the chapel. She looked terrible. She used her same routine in partaking of communion, kissing the host three times, and afterward I spoke to her.

"I'm coming to the end of my life," she said.

"Why do you say that?" I asked.

"I think my time is over. I think my time is over." And as before, she repeated, "I think my time is over."

She went on, talking in what seemed to me like riddles. I wondered what they meant, and I remember going back home and praying that she would disclose more of herself so that I could help her. Then she disappeared for about four or five days, and I discovered she was back in the hospital.

On what would be her deathbed, Mildred told me, "I can't live any longer for only one moment of peace in a life of chaos."

"But Mildred," I protested gently, "no one is saying you're terminally ill. You may need some time in the hospital, but nobody thinks you're dying."

"I'm ready to go home to God," she said.

I gave her communion because I knew how special it was to her. It was a very gentle, quiet time. I saw a softening of her face, and even though I normally don't do this, I laid my hands on her and prayed silently. I prayed that God would be her peace, not a God of confusion but a God of peace. I told her I would return and excused myself.

She died that night. I had asked the hospital to notify me if there was any change in her condition, so I was called, but it was too late. When I arrived at the room, her bed was empty. All the machines had been taken away. There was no one there. Her husband was nowhere to be found, and even if he had been there, I wouldn't have recognized him since we had never met. I remember praying in her empty room that God would bring her eternal peace—not for a moment only, but forever.

I asked a nurse about arrangements, and she referred me to the hospital social worker. When I inquired with her, she said flatly, "There are none."

"What do you mean?" I asked.

"Her husband claimed her body, and there will be no funeral." I offered to conduct a funeral Mass at no expense, but the die had been cast.

"Will there be an interment somewhere?"

"We don't know. Her husband has taken custody of her body."

"Is that it?"

"Yes, her body has already been disposed of."

"Disposed of." I was stunned. Mildred's abuse continued right through her death. I was overwhelmed with the vile nature of evil embodied in another human being. It was so arbitrary, so malicious and vicious. It was beyond belief.

We dedicated one of the daily Mass services to Mildred, but other than that, Mildred simply passed out of existence for many people. My only consolation was that her suffering was over. Later, I remember writing about her. I remembered how her face softened at her last communion. I described my helping her up the stairs and how I—a man—had been allowed to touch her. I am convinced that she experienced some of God's healing that day. In her life, in the midst of all her abuse, she discovered that God could heal her. In her death, Mildred found the gift of peace. It was not parceled out, and no one could take it away from her. It was hers forever.

The prophetic words from the book of Revelation became ever more powerful because of my ministry with Mildred. This is the promise:

> See, the home of God is among mortals.
> He will dwell with them;
> they will be his peoples,
> and God himself will be with them;
> he will wipe every tear from their eyes.
> Death will be no more;
> mourning and crying and pain will be no more,
> for the first things have passed away. (Rev 21:3–4)

Reflection

When a person does not conform to societal and church norms, that person becomes problematic. Far too often we stigmatize nonconformers with labels that are hurtful and demeaning. We simply don't want to engage these persons, initiate a relationship, and know their story. We avoid them and adopt a pattern of tolerance. We condescendingly pray for their betterment. The saints among us are nonconformers. Mildred's life was secure in God, tragic as it was. God was her moment of peace; God embraced her with eternal peace.

Prayer

Lord Jesus, humble us; expose our haughty attitudes and lead us to repent of our judgmental ways. Help us to listen more intentionally to those around us whom we ignore. Lead us to saints in unlikely places, and give us the deep desire to seek out their sacred stories so that they may teach us your ways. Amen.

TOM

The Man Who Had a Tortured Soul

W HEN I MET TOM, he was a retired civil engineer in his late sixties. He had a very angular face with inquisitive eyes and bushy eyebrows. He was divorced—an event that was burned into his psyche. We were introduced by his daughter Beth, who was a member of a different parish, and they met me in the sacristy after Mass. At the time of our introduction to one another, his former wife had been dead for eight years. I subsequently learned that his ex-wife had suffered from severe mental health issues, probably throughout her entire life. She had been hospitalized and went in and out of psychiatric care.

When I first saw him in the sacristy, I remembered that he and his daughter had sat in the second pew—right up front. Tom introduced himself and asked if he could meet for confession, what we now call the Sacrament of Reconciliation.

"Sure," I said.

"Can we meet at my house?" he asked.

"Yes, that will be fine," I replied.

As they were leaving, Beth whispered to me, "He has cancer, and he's dying."

"How long has he had cancer?" I asked.

"Quite a while," she stated. "But now it's really serious. My sister Teresa and I are taking turns caring for him at his house."

I went to Tom's house in the late afternoon, and the other daughter, Teresa, met me at the door. Tom was in the family room waiting for me, and after showing me in, Teresa left the room.

I cannot divulge what Tom told me in his confession, but I can say I learned very little. After we finished, I asked him how things were progressing with his disease. He talked about his chemotherapy and described how the malignancy had spread to his lungs. He said they were checking his liver and his kidneys for spots.

"But that's not what I want to talk about," he said emphatically. "I have a question for you. After I die, will I see my wife? I need to know."

"Why?" I asked.

"Let me tell you our story," he declared.

Tom then began a long account about his wife and her emotional illness. He said that in one of her depressive states she had packed up and moved out. She relocated in another city and decided she wanted to divorce him. According to Tom, she began telling family members that he was abusive and violent.

"But all of that isn't true!" he exclaimed. "It's simply not true! I always loved her."

"Did she love you?" I asked.

"Well, I always wondered about that," Tom responded quietly. "I don't know whether she loved me or not."

I remember thinking that this was one of those situations in which I was hearing only one side of things. It felt like I was walking into someone's head. I had been asked to enter a conversation, and I didn't know where it began and where it ended.

Finally, I asked Tom, "How can I help you? What can I do for you?"

"I want you to talk with me," he said flatly.

So, we set another meeting for the following week. As I left the family room, his daughter Teresa pulled me aside. She walked with me to the front porch where she told me she had heard the end of our conversation.

"Dad's suffering from dementia," Teresa said. "He is living with an illusion that everything between him and Mom was perfect and they had happiness together. Things may have been harmonious at one point, but there was a lot of hurt for both of them. He wanted to be with her forever, but my sister and I know that they hurt each other badly. There were differences on both sides, and the divorce was justified."

I left feeling I was in over my head.

I saw Tom every week at Mass and then every other week at his home. As if the turbulent family dynamics were not enough, my visits with him seemed like a rollercoaster. On my third visit, he looked happy as a lark and told me, "I'm doing wonderfully! Sorry to put you out, but I don't need you today." So, after a brief conversation and prayer, I left.

Two weeks later, Tom was a different person. Rather than meeting me in the family room, he was in his bedroom, lying on his bed but not under the covers. He was fully clothed—no pajamas. I immediately saw Tom's sense of despair.

"I'm guilty of my wife's death," he murmured. "She died of a broken heart that I caused."

He said he wondered if God would judge him and let him into heaven so that he could meet her again. I tried to reassure him of God's love and forgiveness, but I could tell my words were going right by him.

I prayed for Tom at the celebration of the Eucharist, which reminded me of his brokenness.

The next time I saw Tom, he seemed as if he was in a middle place— halfway between despair and euphoria. Actually, I'd describe him as being in la-la land. He was much more pensive. I asked him whether he was on medication for his pain.

"I take the meds the doctor prescribes for me," he quickly replied.

"Will you go back to the doctor soon to have him check up on you?" I asked. He said he would.

"Promise me?"

"Yes."

Then Tom abruptly shifted gears and asked, "What's it going to be like meeting my wife? She died so suddenly."

Actually, I knew from his daughters that her death had been sudden but not unexpected.

Tom asked, "Will she remember me with bitterness about all that we had gone through?"

"Were there bad times?" I asked.

"Yes," he replied. "But I'm trying to understand her bitterness toward me."

I talked with him about how when we meet in the presence of God, we leave our baggage behind. "There is no unfinished business," I told him. Again, I was unsure whether he was hearing me.

Two weeks later, he was back in the hospital, and then he went out of state for treatment. It was a month before I saw him again. This time he was in bed, dressed in a robe and pajamas. He returned to the theme of whether there would be bitterness between him and his wife when they met again. He admitted that there had been a lot of conflict between them during their marriage.

I asked Tom, "Are you praying about this?"

"Yes," he replied. "I'm asking God to give me strength to deal with all this."

"How?" I asked.

"I want to be truthful with her. I want to be honest with her."

"Was this the way you dealt with each other?"

"No, our pattern was deceit."

"What do you think you need to unpack?"

"What really gets to me is that her illness meant everything was focused on her. I have a lot of resentment about that. During our entire marriage, I felt excluded from the marriage. I was physically there, but I really wasn't."

"What else is in your bags?"

"Well, I don't know whether my kids will understand my inability to love her as she was. I need to unpack my unforgiveness of her."

All this time the factual basis of what Tom was telling me was a blur. But gradually his two daughters opened up about their father and his marriage. They told me that it was a conflict-filled relationship almost from day one. It was an abusive marriage. Their father was reactive to everything, especially anything involving his wife. The daughters described him as tense, unpredictable, and frightening. As they got older, they could see the dysfunction even more.

When we met again, Tom was writing. "Who are you writing to?" I asked.

"My wife," he declared. Then he began to read the letter. It was a long, rambling inquiry about their life together. Everything in the letter revolved around their divorce. "How could you do that to me?" he asked. "How could you abandon me?"

I asked him, "How do you feel now?"

"She left me," he muttered. "I was abandoned."

"Do you pray to God about any of this?"

"What does God know that I don't already know?"

"Let me make a suggestion," I said, "I suggest you pray to see your wife, not from your perspective but from God's perspective."

He said he would try.

At our next meeting, Tom told me, "I've tried. God said I didn't see the whole story. God said she was ill. I didn't realize how important that was."

As we talked, it became clear that Tom was more empathetic, rather than resentful. The change was completely amazing to me. God had shown him how to see his wife in an entirely different light.

Before our next meeting, Tom had to be hospitalized. When I saw him again, I was taken aback because he was so thoughtful and reflective. "You know," he said, "I really have been trying to see things from God's point of view. But I can't unpack all this stuff. Maybe I have to take it to God and ask God to unpack it for me."

I immediately thought this was a genuine breakthrough for Tom. Rather than finding his past problematic, he was beginning to see that his past was actually a touchstone for knowing God. As he put it, "God will reveal these things to me."

I saw him for the last time two days before he died. I will never forget the scene. He was lying in bed, and his two daughters sat on either side of the bed. They were showing him family pictures. They were playful with him about the pictures, and even though he lay in bed with sunken cheeks and looked gaunt, he was clearly enjoying this trip through family history. It was fascinating to watch.

At this last meeting, Tom told me, "I'm ready for God to unfold all this. I'm not afraid. I'm actually eager to see what will happen, what's on the other side of life. I think that everything will come home to me when I meet God, and it will finally make sense."

Tom loved to pray the rosary, and he died at home with his daughters praying the rosary.

Tom was one of those tortured souls who approached his death with questions. What is going on? What makes sense in my life? One of the things I have learned is that people always encounter their dying in the midst of their own family dynamics—from childhood throughout the rest of their lives—and so it was with Tom. His failed marriage haunted him, but he finally turned his baggage over to God.

Tom had an intuitive sense that God was there in the midst of his history, but he didn't know how. In his dying, he picked up another tool, another insight—that not everything has to be figured out. From God's perspective, what was uncertain—what he did and did not do—would be made known. Like the Apostle Thomas, Tom yearned for certainty. I believe that he finally reached the point where he could trust God. He died embracing the mystery of not only his own history but also God's love and forgiveness.

Reflection

Fear of the unknown and regret over painful life experiences can torment a person in his or her last journey toward God, especially when laden with a strong scrupulosity. Tom's fear of meeting God and his deep desire to reconcile with his deceased wife consumed his final days. The unknown terrorized him. He struggled with his prayer, hoping that God would understand and forgive his actions. His fear diminished when he finally asked God to view his struggle from God's perspective. God's perspective and peace grew in Tom, and his daughters saw it. And now Tom lives it.

Prayer

God, we need your perspective, your vision, and your compassionate insight for our journey home. Our regrets are heavy burdens. Our fear of the unknown overwhelms us. Enkindle in us a vision of your kingdom and empower us to live its virtues of forgiveness, compassion, and care. Please keep us mindful of your reconciling spirit of love; help us trust you all the time, knowing that darkness is overcome by your great light. Amen.

TERESA

The Woman Who Called Home

I met Teresa in my parish in central New Jersey. She was in her early fifties, and like many in the congregation, she and her family had moved from New York City. Her husband had been transferred by his company, so they were literally suburban transplants. They wanted to fit in, but they didn't quite know how. Teresa and her husband were Italian, and they maintained close contacts with their Italian relatives and friends in "the City." They believed the sun rose and fell on New York City. Teresa had two children, a daughter about sixteen and a son about thirteen.

My first contact with Teresa came as a result of a call from her daughter, who asked that I visit her mother and bring communion. This wasn't entirely unusual, for my first contact with parishioners often comes as a result of home visitation and communion. The daughter said nothing about her mother's illness.

When I arrived at the house, Teresa's husband and children were present. I quickly sensed, and it was later confirmed, that this was a happy marriage and a close-knit family. Teresa was sitting at the kitchen table. She was very pleasant, but I noticed immediately that her hair was covered by a scarf. She looked tired but not really sick.

We met in October, and I learned that they had moved in August. She told me how much they missed New York City and told me that they still went back to the City to go to their butcher, their baker, and their deli. "Where do you find food here?" she asked.

When I gently inquired about her health, Teresa explained that she had had breast cancer five years earlier. The doctors performed a radical mastectomy of her left breast, followed by chemotherapy and radiation therapy. She had received a clean bill of health ever since, but now the cancer had returned. She told me, "I'm totally overwhelmed by this. I've cried and cried. I thought I had beaten it."

I asked her, "How can I be of help to you?"

She replied, "I asked for communion because I need God's strength."

This meeting began a series of visits and phone contacts with Teresa. I discovered that Teresa was very good over the phone. I'm not good with phone conversations, but Teresa was clearly more comfortable on the phone than in face-to-face meetings. She never engaged in any small talk over the phone. She immediately disclosed herself and talked about her deepest fears. This pastoral relationship by phone was very rare for me.

Teresa told me that she didn't want visits from people who would cry or pity her. "I don't want to have to care for other people who think they're caring for me," she said emphatically. So we talked by phone—frequently.

"I'm really concerned about my daughter," Teresa told me. "What impact is this going to have on her? I'm afraid she will be forced to be the caregiver for my husband and son. I know her. She's just like me. She'll want to meet their needs." Over time, I learned that Teresa's concern was legitimate and very real. Her daughter was a caring person and utterly devoted to her mother. When I asked Teresa whether she had shared her concern with her daughter, she said, "Not very much. I don't want to push her into talking about her feelings." Teresa did encourage her daughter to talk with other family members and the school counselor.

Teresa was also very worried about her mother, and this proved to be a powerful factor in the remainder of Teresa's life. Her Italian mother had immigrated to the United States; now in her early eighties, she could only speak Italian. She still lived in New York City, and Teresa talked with her almost daily over the phone.

So there were two dynamics going on here—Teresa and her daughter, and Teresa and her mother.

During one visit, I asked her about her relationship with God, and she explained that she found God mostly through music. I learned that this wasn't necessarily sacred music but Italian operas and folk arias. Teresa told me, "This gives me consolation and a deeper sense of God being with me in my struggles." But, she added, "I still have questions. Why is this happening now? Why did the door close so quickly?"

I often asked her, "Where do you find God in all of this now?" And on one occasion, she surprised me with this answer: "You know, one place I find God is talking to my mother in Italian."

"What is that like?" I probed.

"Well, you know, my mother tells me how much she loves me and cares for me."

"That's where God is," I assured her.

Teresa and her family celebrated their first Christmas in their new home. It was a typical Italian family Christmas. The house was full of people, and there was an absolute barrage of noise throughout the house. There was music, food, laughter, and loud conversations. Teresa came to life during the Christmas holidays.

Then the dark days of January hit, and Teresa became more somber. It was as if her own spirit had been transformed by the weather. She was weary, and she talked a lot more about her fatigue and the burden of her disease. "How is God present in all this?" she asked me.

I replied, "I can't answer how God is present, but I know God is here—with you."

"I know that," she said, "but I'm not feeling it."

Teresa journeyed further into the grey days of winter. She found it increasingly difficult to focus, but she always perked up during phone conversations with her mother. Her mother was occasionally brought to Teresa's house by other family members, but their main contact was by phone. I remember being at the house one time when her mother called. I can't speak much Italian, but I could hear the excitement in her mother's voice because the priest was there and someone was taking care of Teresa.

As Teresa moved closer to hospice care, she returned repeatedly to her worry about how her daughter would deal with her dying, though she never used the words *dying* or *death*. She told me, "I want her to remember the good times we've had."

When hospice was called in, her family moved her from the bedroom to the living room, which meant that they shared all their meals together. Whenever I visited, her favorite music was playing—especially Italian love songs—over speakers placed next to her chair. Her husband told me the music played continuously.

As the cancer progressed, it affected Teresa's voice, which became very weak. She could hardly speak above a stage whisper, and her communication with people declined steadily. During my visits, I would sit next to her or get down on my knees in front of her chaise lounge and simply be with her. She couldn't receive communion because she couldn't swallow, and she couldn't talk to her mother on the phone.

Here is where Teresa's daughter entered the picture. The daughter became a third party to all phone conversations between Teresa and her mother. She knew enough Italian to get by, and when Teresa and her mother talked, Teresa would whisper or write something that the daughter would then communicate to Teresa's mother. She became a bridge between two generations.

Teresa was worried about both her mother and her daughter and how they were handling her dying, but she needed her daughter to communicate with her mother. Her daughter was trying to help both of them, which created an extremely stressful situation for her daughter. I often asked the daughter how she was doing, and most of the time she deflected the question with a typical wave of a teenager's hand. Only once she told me, "I only hope the end is peaceful for her, and I hope it's soon." At the same time, there was something symbiotic about the relationship between these three women, and I was awed by its power.

The day came when Teresa was expected to die. Teresa's voice was gone, but she did not die. Teresa's husband and daughter—and even the hospice workers—began asking each other, "Why is she holding on?" This went on for days.

When I visited Teresa's home, they told me about how she was lingering, and I asked, "When was the last time she's heard her mother's voice over the telephone?"

"Several days," said her daughter.

"I think she needs to talk with her," I said.

So the daughter called the grandmother and told her Teresa was waiting to talk with her. The daughter held the phone, and I sat on the floor next to Teresa's bed. I heard the grandmother say, "Teresa, I love you. Everything will be all right. Everyone will be okay. You can go in peace. I love you."

Teresa mouthed "thank you" and a few moments later she died. It was so quiet and peaceful, and yet so dramatic.

Of all the times I have been with people who were dying, I have never witnessed a greater power of communication than the one between these three generations of women. Teresa was waiting to hear her mother's voice just one last time. Teresa's daughter summed it up so accurately when she told me, "It meant so much to me that Grandma loved my mother the way my mother loved me."

The phone made the crucial difference in Teresa's dying. It became the cement in the relationship of care and undying love. At the very end, Teresa needed to call home.

As I thought about Teresa's dying, I remembered Dvorak's *New World Symphony*, which was appropriate for this tightly knit Italian family living in New York and New Jersey. One movement of the symphony, the *Largo*, was adapted by William Arms Fisher, a pupil of Dvorak's, into a much-loved song called "Goin' Home." Here are Fisher's words:

> Goin' home, goin' home,
> I am goin' home,
> Quiet-like, some still day,
> I am goin' home.
>
> It ain't far, jes' close by,
> Through an open door,
> Work all done, care laid by,
> Goin' t' fear no more.
>
> Mother's there, 'spectin' me,
> Father's waitin' too,
> Lots o' folk gathered there,
> All the friends I knew.
>
> Nothin' lost, all's gain,
> No more fret nor pain,
> No more stumblin' on the way,
> No more longin' for the day.
>
> Mornin' star lights the way,
> Res'less dream all done,
> Shadows gone, break o' day,
> Real life jes' begun.
>
> There's no break, there's no end,
> Jes' a-livin' on,
> Wide awake, with a smile,
> Goin' on and on.
>
> Goin' home, goin' home,
> I am goin' home.
> Here am I, all alone,
> I am goin' home.

Reflection

A house can sometimes become a prison for a critically ill person. It can be confining and uncomfortable, especially as a person loses mobility. But home is different. A home's foundation is built on intimacy and relationships rooted in compassion and unending care. Teresa celebrated life at home. Her disease limited her physical mobility but not the bonds of love between daughter and mother. In the love of three generations of women—grandmother, mother, and child—great care was abundantly evident. In love, the word *God* does not need to be spoken; it is felt, known in a home of tender intimacy.

Prayer

Lord, help us create a home with each other and you. Give us the creativity to listen to your voice in the music that surrounds us, in the stories we tell over and over again, in the photographs that hold powerful memories, and in our prayers that rise up from our hearts to you. Bless us with "calls" from loved ones that send us home to you. Amen.

PAUL

The Man Who Lived for Easter

P AUL WAS A BACHELOR—NEVER married. He had one brother, Sam, who was very close to him in age and who was recently widowed. Paul was a member of my parish, but Sam was not. In his professional life Paul was an accountant, working for corporate clients and toward the end of his career for individuals. He told me that he enjoyed working for individuals and especially liked it when he could do work for senior citizens, whom he did not charge. He also liked to volunteer, and that was how I first met him.

Because I was new to my parish, I decided to check in on the local social services ministry organization, which coordinates mission work in the community on behalf of various congregations. I was met by the executive director, who told me that one of my parishioners, Paul, was there that day. She told me that Paul was very dependable and had been volunteering for years, helping to sort food for the organization's food pantry. But, she added, for the last several years he had experienced health problems. Paul had cancer. It was a brain tumor, and Paul had undergone both radiation and chemotherapy.

I went down the hall and entered a small coffee room with several volunteers. The executive director introduced me to Paul, and I immediately noticed that his head was totally shaved and had a large bandage on it. There was also a large burned area on the side of his head, undoubtedly due to radiation therapy. He wore very thick glasses, and his right eye floated behind the lens. I found this a bit unnerving because it was hard to meet his gaze.

After initial pleasantries, I asked him whether he would like to get together. He said he would appreciate that very much, and I suggested that he phone the parish office and arrange a convenient time for a home visit.

He promised he would. About two weeks later, Paul called and explained that he was going for more tests and probably more treatment. He said he was worried about being wiped out after the treatment and unable to see me. I assured him that I was available whenever he was up to it.

About four or five days later, Paul's brother Sam entered the picture. He called me about Paul. When family members try to tell me how their sick relative is doing, I am wary because I don't know whether the information is accurate. At great length, Sam described his brother, especially Paul's awareness of his sins, and expressed his concern that Paul would eventually be face to face with God. "I don't know how he is going to deal with that," he declared.

I asked Sam, "Has he celebrated the Sacrament of Reconciliation [confession]?"

"Yes, indeed," Sam replied. "But it doesn't seem to do any good. He's obsessed with his sins."

I said, "Do you mean he has a tendency to exaggerate guilt about his sins—what we call 'scrupulosity'?"

"Oh, yes!" Sam exclaimed. "Very much so! Now, you, Father, really need to see him. You have to talk with him. I'll set it up."

At this point I felt very manipulated, but I assured Sam that, whatever happened, I would work with Paul and would welcome a visit with him.

Three or four weeks went by and I heard nothing. Meanwhile, I learned from other parishioners that Paul had undergone another hospitalization and additional treatment. Eventually Sam called and said it was a good time for a visit.

Paul lived in a tired set of condominiums a few blocks from the church. It had two stories and looked more like an aged motel than a building for permanent residents. I walked to Paul's home and met him in his small, one-bedroom unit. Sam was there and immediately excused himself to go to another room.

I asked him, "How are you feeling? From what I know, you must be worn out and drained."

"I'm scared," he answered. "I guess I'm scared about where all this is going."

"Tell me more." As Paul told me details about his disease and treatments, I wondered what his prognosis was.

Eventually he declared, "Well, I know this is going to lead to the end, but I don't want to talk about that."

So I asked him to tell me about his life. He told me about his career as an accountant and how he liked to help people with their financial affairs. "I guess I've been lucky to use my God-given talents for others," he said. He added that he particularly loved his work with the area ministry organization because "I don't work alone. I work with other people." He added that he and his brother were great baseball fans and had season tickets for the area's minor league team.

I gently turned the conversation back to his illness and asked him how he discovered he had cancer. He said it began about five years earlier when he experienced a loss of balance and trouble focusing his eyes. He said his eye trouble was particularly unnerving because he loved to read, especially biographies. His doctor advised him to see some specialists, but he didn't follow through. Then came searing headaches, and he tried treating that with over-the-counter medications. His primary doctor told him that his brain might be involved, and so he underwent a series of tests. Those revealed a stage three brain tumor, and now he was waiting for the results of the latest tests.

I asked Paul, "What do you need from me?"

"I don't know how to handle it," he said.

"'It' meaning dying?" I asked.

"Yes," he replied, "but I don't like to use that term. But yes, that's what I mean."

"I want to walk with you in this," I told Paul, "and I will stay in touch with you."

That first visit with Paul occurred in the late spring when I was making preparations for my fall retreat for people with chronic or terminal illnesses. I advertised the retreat, and one of Paul's closest friends, Martha, told me she thought of Paul immediately. In one of my regular visits with Paul, I suggested that he consider going on the retreat. I had no idea what his response might be.

"This retreat may be a time when God has something important to say to you," I told him, "and it may be an opportunity to hear that."

Paul retorted, "I can't believe God is forgiving me."

I asked, "What's burdening you most? What do you fear?"

"I get the feeling that God may not have forgiven me," Paul replied, gesturing to the large burn on the side of his head but never mentioning his disease.

I said, "God wants you to know his peace and love. Scripture tells us that when God has forgiven sins, they are forgotten. That's God's will. Are you saying you have doubts about that?"

Paul muttered quietly, "My sins have been very bad."

This was a very delicate point in our conversation. I never know how far to push someone in revealing himself. But I went on and asked, "Why would you hold on to your sins when God has forgotten them?"

There was no response. Paul was very quiet; he said not a word.

Finally, I said, "Maybe this retreat has something for you." I left with a huge bag of questions, and in the following days I prayed hard for Paul. I also asked God to guide me: was I pressing too hard—not only for him to talk about his sins but also what I wanted for him in the retreat?

A week later, Sam called and said how beneficial my visit had been. "He's not talking about his sins as much," he reported. "He seems more like himself." I had some doubts about this rosy description, but I let it pass. Sam said the latest test results were ambiguous. Paul's tumor had not grown, but the doctors feared it had spread to other organs.

When I saw Paul again, I noticed he was very quiet and soft-spoken. That was his nature, but this time he was unusually reticent to talk. I could feel the wheels turning in his mind, but nothing was coming out. "You've been processing a great deal of stuff," I suggested.

In a very low voice, Paul said, "I've been thinking a lot. I'm not sure God has forgiven me and forgotten my sins."

"That takes an act of faith," I assured him. "Easier said than done."

"I'm struggling to believe it," he said, and then he abruptly shifted gears. "Tell me about this retreat."

So I described the nature of the retreat and how it affected people. I said, "They come with questions about their relationship with God. They often come with deep doubts. But they frequently come away with the conviction that God loves them and God has forgiven them."

Paul said, "You know my friend Martha. Well, I love her, but she told me, 'You really need to go on this retreat. This is what you must do.' I don't like to be pushed."

I said, "I'm not pushing you. I am offering you an invitation."

I never brought it up again in my regular visits with Paul, but about three months before the fall retreat, Paul told me, "I want my name on the list."

"Why?" I asked.

Paul said, "If this is really happening to me, I have some things I need to pray about, and this may be for me."

Paul went on the retreat in late October. During the retreat I talk to the participants about the prayer of dedicated suffering. Catholics have long taught that people should give up their own suffering to Christ on the cross, but the prayer of dedicated suffering asks God to take their own suffering, transform it into an energy of grace, and then pour it out for another suffering person. After that, we celebrate the adoration of the Blessed Sacrament.[1] When the time came for Paul to pray in the company of the Blessed Sacrament, he immediately began to cry quietly with his eyes closed. I have seen that happen many times but never so quickly. The sacramental presence of Jesus connected with him in a way I never expected. I could feel an energy greater than both of us entering his soul. He held the wafer for a long time, and afterward he said nothing. I didn't ask, but I was so very curious.

At our next meeting in his home, I asked, "What's it been like since you returned from the retreat?"

"I'm free at last," he said. "I'm ready to go."

"Free from what?"

"Free from my questions," he responded, "I gave them to the one who could answer them."

"What happened?"

Paul explained, "It was during the adoration of the Blessed Sacrament. I gave my questions to God." Then followed a long period of silence.

I finally broke through the quiet in the room. "Where are you going now?" I asked.

Paul replied, "I want to prepare for my dying, but I have one request of God. I want to live till Easter."

I quickly calculated that Easter was about four months away. "Why Easter?" I probed.

"Easter is my birthday. That's all I'm asking God."

"Well then," I said, "that's my prayer too. We'll pound the gates of heaven with your request that you live till Easter and your birthday."

I knew that his odds of living until Easter were very poor, and indeed Paul's health declined precipitously after the retreat. But Paul was serene. He was one of those wonderful, nonconfrontational persons with whom the world should be populated one hundred billion times over. He was simply a decent man.

---

1. A prayer service devoted to silence and reflection; see the introduction, xix.

Friends flocked to visit him, and they read to him—poetry, biographies, novels, stories, the Bible, even the church newsletter. They also prayed with him, especially the prayer of the Rosary, which he adored. He also had a little book with a clasp on the cover in which were prayers for all occasions, and Paul frequently asked his guests to read one.

During one of our visits, Paul told me, "I'm finding it difficult to pray. I can't remember what I've said."

I told him, "You don't have to pray the way you have before. Let other people pray for you. Just being silent is a good prayer, and you can trust that God loves you."

Paul said, "Remember the adoration of the Blessed Sacrament on the retreat? Remember what you said about the prayer of dedicated suffering? I pray it for my brother Sam. He's had a lot of losses in his life. He's now a widower. He's had problems in business. And now he's recovering from knee surgery. I pray for him every day."

I was overwhelmed. In his prayer of dedicated suffering, Paul had given up his preoccupation with himself, his scrupulosity about his sins, and his imminent death. Instead, he prayed for his brother. We both started to cry. I told him, "I will pray for your brother Sam too."

Paul's health grew steadily worse, and he went from daily visits from a nurse's aide to round-the-clock care. One day I bumped into his friend, Martha, who told me, "You know what he wants, don't you?" I played dumb. "He wants to live till Easter because that's his birthday." Soon the word was out in the entire congregation, and we all prayed that Paul would live till Easter.

By Holy Week, Paul was unable to communicate at all. His speech was so soft I didn't know what he was saying. He remained at home, and eventually hospice was called in. When I visited him on Good Friday, I thought it would be a miracle if he made it to Easter. I thought about him constantly, particularly his praying for his brother. I kept my cell phone on vibrate wherever I was, and by Easter morning, there was still no call.

Between services on Easter Sunday morning, I walked to Paul's condo. His brother Sam was there. I had brought communion with me. Paul was so weak that he could only twitch his finger. I said, "Paul, it's your birthday. Happy birthday. It's Easter, a day of new life!" He couldn't take communion because he was unable to swallow.

That was the last time I saw Paul. I was convinced he would not last the day, but he actually lived two more days. People continued to visit him until the end, and he died very quietly and peacefully. He simply took a breath, and then that was it.

Paul had made all the arrangements for his death many years earlier. I asked Sam whether he wanted to be involved, but he declined. I mentioned the retreat and asked whether Paul had told him about it. "A little bit," he said.

So I told him about the retreat and the prayer of dedicated suffering. "I need to tell you something," I said. "When Paul prayed, he prayed for you."

His brother started to sob. He cried and cried. I have never seen anyone cry like that. Sam said, "I've always wondered whether Paul was burdened by his guilt and his sins. I'm so relieved that he was freed from that. But," he added, "I can't believe it. He was praying for me. He was praying for me."

The accountant Paul died with the assurance of the Apostle Paul: "In all these things we are more than conquerors through him who loved us. For I am convinced that neither death, nor life, nor angels, nor rulers, nor things present, nor things to come, nor powers, nor height, nor death, nor anything else in all creation will be able to separate us from the love of God in Christ Jesus our Lord" (Rom 8:38–39).

Reflection

Regret for actions in our past is fertile ground for conversion in our life. Our sins oddly become the reference point, the touchstone to receive the tender forgiving embrace of God; confession is good for the soul. For Paul, it was a barrier that had to be overcome, and it became a tool in the hands of God. In this moment of deep, forgiving love, Paul discovered the power to love all over again. It became his mission in his last days to ask God to shower redeeming love upon his brother. He died as he wished, but he found much more—a love and peace that is now his in eternal life.

Prayer

Lord, your love is beyond measure. Our life is not complete until it rests in you. May our journey home reflect your love. Let our prayer gain strength at the cross so that your loving grace may be poured upon all those in need of your compassionate care. Amen.

RACHEL

The Mother Who Lost Her Son

I MET RACHEL EARLY in my ministry when I was a pastor in New Jersey. I was introduced to her by a woman who later helped me start the Gennesaret Retreats.[1] This woman was a nonpracticing registered nurse who was conducting a home visitation ministry, and Rachel was one of the people she saw regularly.

At the time I met Rachel, she was in her late fifties or early sixties. She was a previous cancer survivor, but that was not the issue for her. More problematic was the fact that she had no family. She was completely dependent on other people for everything. She couldn't walk without assistance, and she spent most of her time in a wheelchair. She was extremely limited in what she could do.

The first time I visited her, I was accompanied by my nurse friend. Rachel lived in a small, old, one-level house with a living room, kitchen, bedroom, and bathroom. Almost immediately I had the sense of a woman who was tired and depressed. She didn't smile much, didn't talk much, and certainly didn't talk about her health. Her living conditions matched her inner life. Her house was small and confining. She seemed to be saying, "I'm safe here." Her entire environment seemed comfortably suffocating.

During my first visits, I didn't say much. I simply watched and observed my nurse friend. She would ask Rachel about her family, but there was practically no response. I noticed there were no pictures of children or grandchildren. My friend tried to get her to talk about her husband (we did know she had been married), but that went nowhere. There was nothing in her environment to indicate that she had anyone else in her life. She seemed

---

1. For the story of how the Gennesaret Retreats originated, see the introduction, xvii.

completely separated and removed from other people, except individuals like my friend and me and a few others who brought her food or other supplies.

After about two months of visiting with my friend, one day I asked her if I could have some time to meet with Rachel alone. My friend went out to buy some groceries and run a few errands. I was distressed that Rachel had no photos in her house, so I flat out asked her, "Do you have a family?"

"No," she replied. "I have no family. I used to have a husband. And I had a son."

"Is he alive?"

"Yes."

"Where is he?"

"I don't know."

That was as far as she was willing to go. I thought immediately that there was more to this than she was willing to talk about. I have learned that behind every story there is a backstory, usually a very complicated backstory. So I decided to take another tack.

"Do you go to church?" I asked.

"Well, sometimes someone gives me a ride, but I don't feel I need to go to church very much. I talk to God kind of privately."

"What do you pray for?"

This was met with a long, dreadful silence. I really wanted to take my words back.

Finally, she said quietly and firmly, "You don't want to know what I pray for."

This was obviously a door slamming shut. I thought to myself, "Paul, you don't want to go there." She really wasn't comfortable disclosing herself to me, and I sensed there was a lot of pain in her life. Basically, I thought she was telling me, "It's nice knowing you, but goodbye." When I left, my gut was telling me that here's someone carrying a lot of pain tying her in a knot, but she is not going to open up. I knew all I was getting was little glimpses of her.

I kept in contact with Rachel through visits but also phone calls. Over the phone, she was slightly more open. Her speech would change a bit; it was softer, gentler, and more genuine. I thought there was a sense of trust building between us, but she still would not talk about herself.

During one visit, I asked her, "How can I be of help to you?" The question itself was risky because she refused to acknowledge that she even needed help. For the very first time, she paid me a compliment, and I was floored. This is a terrible thing to say, but because I wasn't getting any feedback, I began to think I could be more useful somewhere else.

Rachel said, "You've already been a great help."

"How?"

"The two of you are the only ones who visit me. You've been a big help by listening to me."

I asked, "If you need something, will you ask me?"

Rachel replied, "If I can, I will."

Behind these cryptic words, I knew there was something going on inside her, something she either could not or would not talk about.

I continued visiting Rachel for about five or six months, usually every three weeks. I saw that her health was deteriorating. Suddenly she was on oxygen for her respiratory illness, but she continued to refuse to talk about her condition. Two months later, as I approached the house, I found the front door unlocked and open. I thought this was very unusual and downright risky, and inside I found her sitting in an easy chair instead of a wheelchair.

"What's going on?" I asked. "What are you doing leaving your door unlocked? Do you do this on a regular basis?"

"It's all right," Rachel said. "I knew you were coming. Besides, this is where I sleep now. I'm not feeling well."

That was the first time I had heard her admit that, and I panicked. "Did you call your doctor?"

"No, but I have his number," Rachel said. "I just need a little more rest."

It was clear that her health was slowly but steadily deteriorating. She looked drawn, and she had lost weight. Despite gentle questioning, she still refused to discuss her situation.

On my next visit, Rachel looked jaundiced, and I was alarmed. "Why don't we call your doctor now?" I said. She weakly agreed—and miracle of miracles, we got through to the doctor immediately. Rachel told him she had a pain in her abdomen. When it seemed she wasn't responding to the doctor, I asked, "Can I help?"

She threw the phone at me—literally. I picked it up and described her yellow color to the doctor. He told me Rachel had a hard time accepting medical care and he was worried about dehydration and her kidney function. He wanted her to come to the hospital immediately, so I drove her the short distance to the emergency room.

After getting her settled there, I met the doctor, who admitted her to the hospital. "I'll know more in the morning," he said, and then he asked, "Is there any family?" I replied that I thought there was a son, and he admitted he had never heard her speak of any family.

Rachel stayed in the hospital for two days of tests. I visited her and discovered that the doctor had diagnosed the pain in her abdomen as a malignant tumor affecting her stomach and pancreas. The doctor told me the options were radiation or surgery, and it was a very delicate operation to remove the tumor. Everything I came to know about her condition I learned from her doctor. Rachel still refused to talk about her situation. The doctor, clearly worried about a malpractice claim, pressed me about her family, and all I could tell him was that I thought there was a son.

At this point, Cathy, the lay Catholic chaplain at the hospital, entered the picture. I knew her from a previous parish, and we had been friends for several years. She began visiting Rachel, so now there were three of us caring for Rachel—a hospital chaplain, a parishioner, and me. I asked Cathy whether Rachel had ever mentioned her son. Cathy told me Rachel had talked about a child, but not specifically a son.

Meanwhile, the doctor was pressing us about finding a family member to approve the next steps in Rachel's care. We tried to get Rachel to talk about her son, and eventually she told us that he was living in northern New Jersey. She said she had an old address and phone number for him, but it was at home. My nurse friend retrieved the address book. Cathy repeatedly attempted to reach him. The calls went unanswered.

One day the three of us went to visit Rachel. When we entered, she asked my friend and Cathy to leave. In a weak voice, she told me, "About my son. We had a knock-down, drag-out fight about a terrible thing. That was six years ago. I've felt guilty about it ever since. I tried to contact him, but I got no response."

I said I knew that was painful, but that's as far as she would go. I explained that the doctor really needed permission to proceed with her treatment. She barely acknowledged that. So I told the doctor, and he decided to go ahead with radiation therapy, which wiped her out. The radiation produced some reduction of the tumor but nothing significant. Even worse, the tumor began pressing on other organs, and the doctor recommended surgery. Rachel gave him an emphatic no. She was not mentally deranged and was fully conscious of her condition. She simply refused.

Rachel was then discharged from the hospital and went home. She received home care from visiting nurses, and the doctor stayed in touch with her by phone and even visited her once at home. When I was with her, I asked, "Why did you refuse surgery?"

"What's the use?" she retorted. "What is there to live for?"

"What about your son?" I asked.

"No, I just want to die."

"That sounds so despairing."

"That's what I've decided."

Rachel went steadily downhill. She was readmitted to the hospital and was placed in acute, long-term care where she could stay for an extended period. Soon the staff started palliative care. After about a week, I asked her, "What's the purpose of this?"

"I'm waiting for him to call me." (She always referred to her son as "him," never by his name.)

"What if he never calls?" I asked.

"Then that's the way I'll die."

The doctor told me that if she survived two weeks, it would be a miracle. Instead, she lived six weeks. The son never called. The three of us basically became her family, and we visited Rachel together quite often.

On the day she died, I remember that the three of us held hands around her bed. We were all crying. She lost consciousness, and I put my hands on her. About an hour later, she breathed her last.

I remember I was angry—really angry. I was angry because Rachel wouldn't tell me about herself or her son. I was angry because of the way she died—so alone. Her physical condition was actually a by-product of the trauma in her life. She had lost her son. Her heart was broken; her life spirit had gone out of her. At the moment of her trauma with her son, she literally stopped living.

I never learned what alienated Rachel and her son. But I gradually realized that my need to know and my frustration with her refusal to disclose herself were beside the point. She had gone as far as she was willing to go.

Her death was, without doubt, one of the saddest moments in my ministry. Since then, I have seen that her consolation in the midst of great suffering came from the few people who would not abandon her. She was a gift to us. Rachel taught me that each person's journey and pain are her own. As much as I had a desire to know, it was her life and her burden. She carried it with patience and a longing for a reunion that never happened. I can't blame her son; I don't know what had happened years earlier. But it's very hard to see the tragedy of two people who are estranged and never talking, and then one of them dies. It reminds me of the prophet Jeremiah, who wrote,

> Rachel is weeping for her children;
> she refuses to be comforted for her children,
> because they are no more. (Jer 31:15)

I pray for Rachel and her son, even to this day, for I am convinced that in God's presence, they will find each other again. I am sure that her comfort now rests with God alone.

Reflection

No one should underestimate the value of his or her relationship with anyone else. None of us can know what impact we have had on another person. We should not be surprised to discover that something we said or a wish yet to be fulfilled may keep a person waiting expectantly for our return. Rachel waited for her son so that she might apologize to him. The years of alienation locked them out from each other. She died waiting for her son with her apology in her heart—a lonely way to die.

Prayer

Lord, give us a deep awareness of our finiteness. Time is not unlimited, and opportunities will expire. Give us the courage and determination to express our regrets promptly and expel our resentments quickly. We know your love sets us on a course of reconciliation. Send us your Spirit to fill us with grace as we reach out to those we have injured. May your peace surround us. Amen.

JOEY

The Man Who Died with the Hope
of God as the Good Shepherd

I MET JOEY IN 1986. I had left Saint Meinrad Seminary and returned to parish work at in New Jersey. Part of my pastoral responsibility was visiting the sick at the nearby hospital. I was close friends with the hospital chaplain, Elizabeth, and she was completing her supervision for Clinical Pastoral Education accreditation at another hospital. Elizabeth's CPE supervisor suggested that she see Joey.

Elizabeth had a long talk with him. She discovered that he was a young man who had drifted away from the church. He told her he had lived a promiscuous lifestyle, and he said he wanted to visit with a priest—"someone I can talk to." That's when she contacted me.

"What does he want?" I asked her. "What does he need?"

Elizabeth replied, "I think he's looking for someone who is not judgmental." She never used the term "AIDS." She said he had a chronic illness. "You may not have heard of it," she said. "On the street, they call it 'the gay cancer.'"

Joey was only twenty-nine years old. It's important to remember that this was the early stage of all the hysteria about AIDS. It was often called "the gay plague," and this was my very first encounter with someone who had AIDS. I had read about it, but I was really ignorant. All I knew is that it was a sexually transmitted disease.

Elizabeth and I met a few days later and went to his room. It was very dark. The blinds and curtains were closed. There was only a dim light over his bed. He was asleep.

My very first impression of him was how emaciated he was. His face was drawn, and he had deep, sunken cheeks. He had thick, black hair and very dark eyebrows. He looked malnourished, and he was very weak that day.

Elizabeth introduced me and then excused herself. I sat down in a chair so I could be at eye level with Joey. I gave him a brief, open-ended introduction of myself and told him I would try to be of whatever help he needed.

Joey said, "I don't really know where to begin because I don't know what I want to tell you and what I don't want to tell you."

"I'm here to listen," I assured him. "You can tell me anything you're comfortable with."

Joey began to tell me his personal history. He spoke in a very hesitant, halting way because he was so weak. He told me he had been born in New Jersey and raised there as one of four children. He had two older brothers and one younger sister, and they were very close in age. He and his siblings had attended Catholic schools, but when they went to college, they split in different directions.

Joey said he loved art. He was also very good in math, so he thought he would combine his skill in drawing and aptitude in math and study architecture. He ended up at the University of California, Berkeley.

While Joey was still in high school, he came out and told his parents of his homosexuality. He said he had been aware of his attraction to men even in his preteen years. His family's reaction was pretty much unfavorable. "It wasn't a verbal battle," he said. "They were mainly shocked and disappointed." He said that they were more concerned about what they would say to other family members and friends. "Basically, my father and brothers were very negative," he reported. "My mother has been very consoling, but she doesn't really understand me. My sister is the only one who has embraced me and been very supportive."

Joey said that he hung around with the art and theater students in high school and began experimenting sexually during his last two years in high school. I figured this meant he had been sexually active for about sixteen years. Finally, he said, "I'm too tired to go on, but there's more to tell."

I promised to visit him weekly, and that was the end of our first session.

Our second session was very strange. It was a conversation while he was undergoing a radiation treatment for his condition. It was a grueling bombardment of heavy radiation. He was isolated in a private room that I could not enter. Instead, I was in an adjoining room, and the only way we could talk was via phone. It was a perfect example of his isolation, spiritually and relationally.

Joey resumed his story, telling me that when he entered Berkeley, he was quickly swept up in a very promiscuous lifestyle. This included sex with strangers, and it was pretty much what other people were doing at that time. During the early eighties, there was a bitter battle between people who believed that AIDS wasn't real and those who believed it was a danger but wanted to use it to change homosexuals. This debate fueled the promiscuous lifestyle of gay people. "Looking back," Joey reflected, "I realize that my conduct was potentially so malicious that others might be dying now."

That was the end of our relatively brief conversation by phone. The next time we spoke face to face. Joey began to cry almost immediately. Between his sobs, he expressed deep, deep remorse. But along with his regrets emerged a powerful sense of anger. "I know my lifestyle wasn't good," he said, "but society is so hostile toward us. They're afraid of us, and they hate us. And I'm just as angry with God."

"Can you say more about that?" I asked.

Joey responded, "When I was growing up, I thought God would take care of me. Then I became aware that I was attracted to men, and that was pretty scary. So I began looking for something to hang on to. In our church there was a statue of Jesus as the Good Shepherd. That made me believe I could go to this person, so I talked to him in that way, knowing that I was safe with him."

Then Joey shifted, and the anger poured out. "That God is now gone," he muttered. "God is really a vindictive, judgmental God. He is condemning me, and if I die, I'm going to be eternally lost."

That immediately put me on the defensive, and I felt like saying that God wasn't like that—God *wasn't* judgmental. God is a loving and gracious God. But I squelched my rebuttal. Our conversation ended on that note, and I left him with his anger and sadness.

The next day Elizabeth, the chaplain, told me that Joey wanted to see me again. She gave me his number, so I phoned him. He was all apologetic. "I'm sorry about what I said about God," he declared. "I really am sorry. That probably upset you, and I didn't want to do that."

I didn't know what to say, but I told him, "That's all right. No apology is needed."

"Will you come back?" Joey asked.

"Of course I will. I'll see you Tuesday."

At our next meeting, he started apologizing all over again. I batted that down pretty quickly and told him I was there to listen and to be with him. But I did feel it was necessary to confront him, so I said, "Last time you were so angry with God and your family. Why didn't you tell me to get the hell out and never come back?"

Joey was very, very quiet. This lasted a long time. He never responded to my question. Instead, he went deeper into his life story. He told me about a man he had lived with. He never called him his partner, and he said they had an open relationship that included sexual encounters with many others. Joey said, "I wonder if I acquired AIDS from him."

"Why is that important?" I asked.

"Well, maybe I passed it along without knowing it. Maybe if I got it from him, I would feel less guilty about my relationships with other men."

"Would that make a difference or change your relationship with God?"

"Probably not," Joey sighed. "I'm grasping at straws. I want something to hold on to."

During this visit, Joey looked more and more ragged. When I asked him about his friends and family, he said a few of his friends had visited but only very briefly. One of his brothers had come to see him a couple of times, but the other brother and his father never came. Only his mother and his sister visited regularly.

"I tried to talk to my mother about my funeral," he said, "but that literally drove her out of the room. She cried and said she didn't want to talk about that. So I've been talking with my sister. She's the one who's helping me with my funeral plans. But I'm convinced that the church won't bury me because of my lifestyle."

I told him, "That would be highly unusual unless you contacted a priest who wouldn't be predisposed toward you anyway."

With that advice, Joey asked his sister to find a church and a priest who would bury him.

At our next visit, Joey announced that he wanted to talk about his funeral. He was holding a piece of paper, and on it he had drawn a circular image, something like a mandala. "I want this used on the bulletin for my funeral," he explained. "It gives me a sense of wholeness. It symbolizes me in one place, and I'm offering myself to God."

"What happened to the God who is so vengeful?" I asked.

"I'm not finished with that," Joey said. "I'm still angry with that God, but I remember my earlier image of God as a loving God. This is my offering to the loving God who will embrace me and take care of me."

We talked about that at length, and Joey referred to some Scripture passages he wanted read at his funeral. This was the first time I sensed in him an acceptance of himself at a very deep level; he was not beating himself up. I had a glimpse of him moving in another direction.

That visit took place in mid-October, and he died in early December. I had started seeing him in September, so this was about halfway to his death. Joey knew he would lose the power to communicate, so he asked me to take notes and leave the notes for his sister at the hospital. I also gave his sister my phone number so that she could call me.

As death approached, Joey wanted to go home. The hospital advised against it. His parents were reluctant to hire hospice, and a battle broke out among his family members over how to take care of him. His sister, who was his strongest ally, volunteered to take care of him at his parents' home despite their deep reluctance to have him return.

On my last visit with him before he went home, he said, "Will you pray for me?"

When someone asks me that, I am always unsure of what to say. "What do you want me to pray?" I asked Joey. "What's your deepest desire?"

Joey replied, "I want to be received at home with kindness. I want to be as kind to my family as they are to me. I want those days to be filled with kindness and peace."

I touched his hand very gently because I knew he was in great pain. I prayed that Joey would know kindness and peace from his family, and after praying with him I offered him the Sacrament of Reconciliation (confession). He agreed and received it.

I left with the gut feeling I wouldn't see Joey again and the end was closer than he thought. Three weeks later Joey called and asked me to come for a final visit. "I want you to meet my parents," he said.

I agreed to come, and when I arrived, his sister, one of his brothers, and his parents greeted me very kindly and graciously. His parents looked tormented and exhausted. I asked for some time alone with Joey, and they left the room.

Joey looked very weak. I didn't stay long, and I prayed quietly with him. Before I blessed him, Joey motioned me to come closer. I bent over so that my ear was next to his mouth. He whispered, "Thank you."

I went out of the room. This was the first time I had met his parents, and they had a ton of questions. It was a difficult conversation. They bombarded me with all sorts of issues about the church and about what they should tell people about how Joey died. I sympathized with them because at that point that's how most people acted when dealing with AIDS. But this was such a disjuncture with what I had just experienced with Joey that I almost said I couldn't help them. I didn't know their priest, so I suggested various possibilities for referral. They told me they knew Joey had some plans for his funeral, but I got the impression they would not follow through and would somehow modify them. As I left, I told his sister to call me if I could help.

Just before Thanksgiving, his sister called to report that she had found a church and a priest who could do the funeral. She asked, "Could you preach?"

I responded tentatively. "Are your parents okay with that? You know, funerals aren't for the deceased."

"Yes, they're fine with that," she stated.

So I agreed. Joey died in early December, and at his funeral I preached on one of the texts Joey had selected. It was from John 14: "Do not let your hearts be troubled. Believe in God, believe also in me." It was ironic because everyone there was troubled and overwhelmed by what had happened.

I didn't know what to say except that Joey had taught me a great deal about how someone could own his life in all its complexity, pain, and confusion. I told them about Joey's two images of God—the judgmental and vindictive God and the kind and merciful God. I thought Joey would have wanted me to say that. I said, "Joey ended his life with the hope of being met by the Good Shepherd God who would welcome him home."

We buried Joey on a gray, rainy day. His was a single grave, not part of a family plot, and that said something about Joey and his family. Even in death, he was separated from them.

Joey died at such a young age. I always wondered what his life might have become. I think he was the kind of person who would have been very likable. He didn't die without anger toward God, and part of him believed that God was still judging him. But he also died in the hope of being embraced by the Good Shepherd. He died in peace, knowing that was true.

I never told anyone at my parish about my ministry with Joey. It wasn't their business. I figured it was my ministry.

Reflection

Joey's suffering under the specter of death was overwhelming and isolating, creating a barrier in his relationships with family, friends, and God. This isolation is formidable but not impenetrable. Yet, each day a hunger grew within him for acceptance and forgiveness from God. This is the gift of faith, a covenant of hope borne in the compassionate heart of God for everyone.

Prayer

Lord, keep our hearts rooted in you; in our suffering give us hope, in our companionship with our loved ones give us strength. Lead us by your spirit, to create a listening heart within us that allows us to hear your voice in our dying, so that we can live forever in your loving, tender embrace. Amen.

ROSA

The Woman Who Lived in Joy

R OSA WAS FROM PUERTO Rico. I met her through Bob, my best friend and fellow priest. Rosa was a member of Bob's parish. She was in her early sixties, and she had been diagnosed with breast cancer ten years earlier. The cancer went into remission, but now it had returned and metastasized in her kidneys, liver, and bones.

She and her husband attended Mass at Bob's church, and she learned about my Gennesaret Retreats through a flyer in the Sunday bulletin. She told Bob that she had read about the retreat, but she wasn't sure she was sick enough. She waited a year, and when her condition grew worse, she decided to apply for the retreat.

I went to Rosa's home to interview her for a spiritual assessment as part of the admissions process. She had been previously interviewed by the retreat nurse coordinator who obtained an up-to-date medical history. The nurse coordinator spoke very highly of her and her fitness for the retreat.

Rosa lived in a tiny house; they were obviously poor. She was a lovely woman and very much alive. The first thing she said to me was this: "You're not from Louisville, are you?"

"No," I said, "I'm from New Jersey."

"New Jersey!" she exclaimed. "That's where we're from!"

What followed was a lively conversation about New Jersey, where I was born and where I had served as a priest. When she heard that my cousin was a priest in Freehold, where she had lived before moving to Louisville, she shouted, "I know him!" Rosa explained that she and her husband were part of a Catholic parish in New Jersey, which I knew was a charismatic renewal parish. They still had a lot of family back in New Jersey, and they stayed in close touch. Her husband had been transferred to Louisville by GE. Like so many transplanted Easterners, Rosa wanted to know, "Where can you find food here? Where's the deli? Where's the bread?" We hit it off right away.

Rosa was vivacious. She had an infectious smile that made her face come alive. She was now a homemaker, but in New Jersey she had done some factory work. She was very handy, and she was skilled as a seamstress, which bonded her to some other women in her neighborhood.

When I asked, Rosa told me about her illness. She said it was very unexpected. "It totally surprised me," she said. When I asked her what she was carrying to the retreat, she told me that she wondered whether she would have enough strength to deal with her suffering. Then she poured out the story of her life. She was firmly confident that God would provide her with the strength she needed for this final journey. She knew that Jesus loved her. She said that she was desperately concerned about the future of her family. This was her second husband. Her first husband was an alcoholic and abused her. They divorced. They had three children, two of whom were married. The third—a son—was in his early twenties and single. Nominally living with them, he was in and out of the house. Rosa said she was very concerned about him. "I'm not sure he will make it through this," she said, but added, "I don't think he would do anything harmful to himself." I didn't know whether this might be a reference to alcohol or drugs, and I never found out. Whenever I encountered the son on my visits, he never gave me the time of day.

I wondered whether she and her husband had been married in the church. An annulment of her first marriage in a church tribunal would probably have been available to her, but that was a decision for her and her pastor to make. I did know that she loved her priest and that she and her husband commuted a long distance each weekend to go to Mass. They also contributed money to the parish, although they clearly couldn't afford to do so.

Rosa joined us on the retreat. The single most important event for her was the adoration of the Blessed Sacrament and the time of silent prayer that followed.[1] During this extended period of personal prayer while holding the Blessed Sacrament, she burst into tears. Later, she explained to me: "My tears were my relief that God was close to me and I was close to him. I felt his peace; I am now at peace."

---

1. A prayer service devoted to silence and reflection; see the introduction, xix.

Her retreat experience became her strength. After the retreat, she declined steadily and dramatically. Although she was hospitalized once, she returned home and hospice was called in.

As her health worsened, I frequently visited Rosa in her home. The atmosphere was so Latin it was unbelievable. Jorge, her husband, literally hugged you into the house. Their welcoming love was tangible. Their house was very small, but it seemed to be bursting with their affection for one another.

When I visit very sick people, I am very respectful of their beds. The bed is the last place where they still have control, so I never sit on it unless I am invited to do so. I always take my cue from others in the room.

On one of my last visits with Rosa, I immediately saw two things. First, Jorge and the older daughters were very close to her at the top of the bed. As they talked with Rosa, they stroked her hair and touched her forehead. Second, Rosa's son stood at the end of the bed with his back against the wall. Everyone else was close to Rosa, and her son's estrangement was obvious. He seemed to be saying it was a deathbed, and he clearly didn't know how to handle the situation.

Rosa, however, was radiant. When she smiled, the people around her melted, and she smiled until she died. In one sense, you would never have known that she was sick. She was very attentive to others, rather than herself, and she hugged you into her family. She brought you to herself. Before the retreat, she was fearful and anxious about her family and the future, but the retreat had changed her inside out.

Praying with Rosa was a natural moment. Often it was just the two of us, and often Rosa led, using prayers and songs from her charismatic background. She never prayed in tongues, but her prayers were very personal and powerful. It was a remarkable witness to the power of God to sustain her and give her comfort. She never lost a sense of the comfort of God in the true meaning of that word, *comfort*—"to be with." She truly believed in the joy and power of God, and she lived it from her bed.

As Rosa declined, her son was clearly struggling. His estrangement was obvious, so I asked Rosa, "Can I help in some way?"

She said, "No, he has to work this through by himself."

I visited Rosa on the day she died. Everyone was there—her husband Jorge, her two daughters, and her son. They were praying and singing in Spanish as I held Rosa's hand. Her son approached the bed, but never quite touched it. Finally, as death came closer, he came to the foot of the bed, sat down and leaned forward, almost lying and touching his mother.

I prayed the prayers of commendation, which surrendered Rosa to God. As she died, she was very quiet. There was no heavy breathing, no struggle. She died at peace. When she breathed her last, we did not notice it.

Afterward, Jorge tried to be strong for everyone but soon broke down in tears. One of the daughters lay next to her mother, crying softly. Her son sat on the bed, his body wracked by deep sobs. I put my hand on his shoulder for several minutes, and then he got up and walked away without a word.

I wanted to conduct the funeral, but Rosa had earlier decided that she wanted her funeral in New Jersey at her beloved Catholic charismatic parish. I quickly discovered how complicated the arrangements could be when a casket has to be shipped to another state. The family spent six anxious days making the arrangements, which were further complicated by a lack of money. I contacted a priest friend in New Jersey who took care of Rosa's family and the funeral arrangements. Eventually their extended family network contributed the money to transport the body for burial.

The funeral home in New Jersey provided what are called "remembrance cards," and on the back of Rosa's card was a poem that spoke of her spirit:

> I'd like the memory of me
> to be a happy one.
> I'd like to leave an afterglow
> of smiles when life is done.
> I'd like to leave an echo
> whispering softly down the ways,
> of happy times and laughing times
> and bright and sunny days.
> I'd like the tears of those who grieve
> to dry before the sun
> of happy memories that I leave
> when life is done.

Rosa's joy in life was also a joy in dying. Though sometimes hard to understand and accept, the words of the letter of James capture her life and dying: "My brothers and sisters, whenever you face trials of any kind, consider it nothing but joy, because you know that the testing of your faith produces endurance; and let endurance have its full effect, so that you may be mature and complete, lacking in nothing" (Jas 1:2–4).

Rosa considered her life nothing but joy. In the midst of great suffering and anxiety about her family, she found peace forever.

Reflection

Rosa was a stranger in a strange land in more ways than one. Her familiar church family was hundreds of miles away. Her homeland was farther still. She spoke a second language—English—while firmly believing that God heard every language of prayer; her prayer was written in the language of the heart, lover to lover. Cancer was not the enemy; it was an opportunity to be with God. Her enemy was concern, worry, and anxiety about her family; they too were now in a very strange new land. She knew that everyone she cared for had to live in this new land on their own. She trusted that God would provide the means for them.

Prayer

Lord, help us to do what sounds simple; help us to let go of whatever holds us hostage so that you may take action. Help us to let go and let you be the God of our lives. Make us aware that our loved ones are in your care, for you never abandon them. Give them a new vision to see you—new hearing to notice your voice, and a new heart to trust in your love for them. Lead them to your kingdom and eternal peace! Amen.

CHARLIE

My Brother

I HAVE VERY STRONG feelings about this story about my brother Charlie because he died just a few weeks before my telling it. This is less a story about my ministry than an account of a man who lived in faith—one day at a time.

Charlie was the only child born to my parents; my sister and I were adopted, and Charlie came along later as a surprise. He was called "the miracle child." His birth in 1952 was a remarkable event, and since children weren't allowed in hospitals at that time, I remember vividly standing outside the hospital and waving to my mother who was standing at a window, holding Charlie in her arms. It was a difficult birth for my mother, who had previously been unable to carry a baby to term.

Charlie was a happy kid with a very even temperament. He was one of those people who could level mountains and fill in valleys. He was also extremely bright, and like his father he was good with figures.

In late grade school or early high school, Charlie developed the first of several health problems that would plague him the rest of his life. He played football, and even though he didn't excel at it, he was committed to the team and the game. He injured his hip and had some medical treatment, and also went to a chiropractor for what were called "adjustments." Nothing really worked, and he lived with his injury for the rest of his life. Charlie's early hip injury was a metaphor for the rest of his life. He didn't limp, but everything was always out of place.

His later illnesses, which ran in both my father's and mother's families, included heart disease, diabetes, cancer, and arthritis. He was a miracle child who was plagued by family diseases, but he carried them with patience and courage.

All of us Scaglione children went through the Catholic schools. For college, Charlie attended St. Joseph's University in Philadelphia, where he majored in accounting. In college he met his future wife, Dale, and their relationship moved fairly quickly toward marriage. She was the daughter of a minister in the Reformed Church in America. His future father-in-law assured him that one church was as good as another; it was his relationship with Christ that was central. But this Protestant–Catholic marriage was a source of great consternation to my Italian Catholic parents and their family. For lifelong Catholics, their marriage was hard to swallow.

When it came time for them to be married, Charlie asked me to participate in the wedding. By that time I had been ordained, and I explained that I could not perform a wedding that the church had not sanctioned. But, I added, I could do it if he applied for permission to be married outside the church. He did that, and I participated in the service.

Dale and Charlie were married in a small, quaint Reformed church in a little town in the Catskills. His father-in-law officiated. The members of his congregation were teetotalers, and this presented huge problems for the Italian Catholics who attended. So, on the day of the wedding, there were two receptions. One was in the parish hall and featured finger foods and punch and no music or dancing. The Italian Catholics had rented a bus to come to the wedding, so there was a second reception on the bus, featuring alcohol and all kinds of food and plenty of loud music. Neither group could believe what was happening. It was one of the most bizarre things I have ever seen.

Charlie connected with his wife's family, especially his father-in-law. I could see that he was becoming more evangelical—what he described as "putting a face on Christ." I think he found there a personal relationship with Christ that he didn't find in his Catholic tradition, and that was hard for me to understand since I have a strong personal relationship with Christ.

Faith became absolutely central to his family life. Charlie and his wife joined a congregation associated with the Christian and Missionary Alliance, a denomination with roots in New York State. It was a missionary-minded church, and Charlie and Dale made missionary trips to Mexico with their two children, David and Joy Marie.

Charlie worked in a very responsible, high-paying job as an internal auditor with IBM in Poughkeepsie, and after turning down numerous transfers, he finally relented and the family moved to Raleigh, North Carolina.

During one of their mission trips to Mexico, Charlie for the first time had what was eventually diagnosed as a heart attack. He attributed his distress to the altitude in Mexico, but on returning to Raleigh, the doctors told him that he had three blocked arteries and needed open heart surgery. He was thirty-three.

It was a long operation—six or seven hours. Afterward, he was in the intensive care unit, and Dale and I were allowed to visit separately for only ten minutes at a time. Charlie lay there, intubated and unable to move. He could wiggle his right thumb and first finger, so the only communication from him came through touching.

Charlie's heart surgery was a major event in my faith and belief. Here was my younger brother, thirty-three years old with a wife and two children. I couldn't understand why this was happening to him. How could God allow this? I wanted to be there for my brother, but I knew I couldn't be present for him in the same way that I could be for my Catholic parishioners. All my sacramental options simply weren't available to me.

I sensed a great distance between my brother and me, and that experience has become very important to me in the rest of my ministry. I couldn't understand Charlie's suffering, but I also couldn't leave him. I have come to realize repeatedly that as close as I am to people who are dying, there is a great personal gulf between that person and everyone else. It's almost like watching a balloon on a long string: you hold on to the string, but you know that eventually all that string will run out and the balloon will take off on its own.

How can you be with people who are suffering? It's not uncommon for me to cry, but often I do that later. When I am with them, it feels sacred simply to be in the same space with them. I have to recognize that I do not have power. It's very humbling to minister in that space.

I've never liked people who say, "I was just with him," as if "just being there" was nothing. I think it's everything. Charlie and I communicated by touching, and the contact, the touching, was enough. He knew my presence even though I could not know his suffering. That has always been a great, wonderful mystery God has given me in this ministry.

Charlie's surgery was very complicated. I later learned he was left with about 30 percent heart function, which is pretty low. The doctors predicted a slow recovery.

Charlie was very faithful about his rehab program, and gradually he regained strength.

When he got home, I called him and asked, "How are you doing?"

Charlie said simply, "Okay."

I probed a bit further. "How are you feeling about this?"

"Well, the doctors told me the bypasses are good, and I will have a good life."

I wondered about his spiritual life and whether this experience had affected it at all, but I knew I was his brother, not his pastor. At the same time, I wanted him to feel that he could talk to me about his spiritual life and wanted to encourage him to do that. He assured me he was okay and declared, "I prayed before surgery and left everything in the hands of God. I knew God would take care of me." I couldn't argue with that and left it alone.

Charlie never revealed details about his health. We later learned that his prognosis after surgery wasn't very good, but he actually lived pretty well. He returned to work, and he worked very hard, sometimes eighteen hours a day. He never complained.

Suddenly he was trapped in a downsizing at IBM and lost his position. He was devastated. "IBM—I've Been Moved, *out*," he quipped bitterly. Losing his job put him and his family in a precarious position financially, especially now that they were without health insurance. He was always three steps ahead of himself, and perhaps he had some sense of what might happen to him. I found out only the year he died that before his heart surgery, he had taken out health insurance policies on his wife and two children.

After leaving IBM, Charlie organized his own computer company, focused on information technology. At first it was successful, but later it fell apart. Charlie was deeply disappointed, but at the same time he was connecting with the University of South Carolina, where he worked for the rest of his life.

Charlie's health began to deteriorate, and now he suffered from a rapid heartbeat. His heart rate would inexplicably soar into the hundreds. Doctors implanted a device similar to a pacemaker, but he had problems. A couple of these units shorted out entirely. He was suffering from ongoing congestive heart failure, and his heart tissue was deteriorating.

Charlie dealt with this heart condition for the rest of his life. His cardiologist prepared a file on him, and it grew so large that it filled two five-inch binders. The file was so big that when he was in the hospital, it was simply left outside his door rather than on a shelf.

When I would ask him how he was doing, he would quote Scripture, then say, "God doesn't give you more than you can bear. I trust God more than I trust myself." That was the theme I would hear from Charlie for the rest of his life. It was his mantra.

In the midst of his heart problems, he noticed nodules on his breast and in his armpit. He had breast cancer, and it had spread to his lymph nodes. Breast cancer is extremely rare in males, and it hit Charlie when he was about forty. He had surgery, plus radiation and chemotherapy, which made him very sick. "Heart surgery felt like an elephant sitting on my chest," he told me, "but I'd rather have that than chemotherapy."

The next chapter in Charlie's health history involved hip and knee problems. In his hip, bone rubbed against bone. He had hip surgery, which was actually a repair of his boyhood treatment. He couldn't exercise, and so he began to gain weight. He became a borderline diabetic and was eventually diagnosed with type 2 diabetes.

By his early forties, Charlie had multiple illnesses—heart disease, breast cancer, hip problems, diabetes. Every ailment had a ripple effect. To make matters worse, his doctors didn't always consult with one another, which proved to be a problem until his death.

When I would ask him, "How are you?" he would often reply, "What part of me?" That kind of humor kept him sane. He could have thrown up his hands in utter despair at his situation. Or, like some people, he could have blamed God. Not Charlie. He suffered through several hospitalizations, but he bounced back with a resilient spirit. This wasn't just rolling with the punches. He had a profound trust that the time he had been given by God was given to him for a purpose, even if that purpose would be disclosed only gradually or intermittently. Because of his personal relationship with Christ, he literally lived one day at a time. His spirituality gave him the awareness that through Christ, he could handle whatever happened.

After his breast cancer surgery, the doctors told Charlie that the malignancy might reappear in another form, probably as bone cancer. There was no treatment for that, only pain management and medication to slow its progress. That's what happened to Charlie. He was working as the grant coordinator in the School of Engineering at the University of South Carolina, supervising federal grants for fuel cell battery development and doing fairly well. He began experiencing pain in his right leg, which wasn't related to his hip problem, and two years before he died, he was told he had bone cancer.

Charlie had radiation therapy to slow the growth of the malignancy and more painful hospitalizations. His other diseases flared up. Treating one problem would exacerbate his other illnesses.

About a year before he died, Charlie said to me in passing that it might be good for him, my sister, and me to get together and reminisce. Charlie never asked things for himself. He was always upbeat but never directed attention toward himself. But I missed this signal from him, and the three Scaglione children never did get together before his death.

The last time I saw Charlie was a few months before he died. He came to see me in Louisville despite my protesting that he shouldn't make the trip. Fortunately, his daughter did much of the driving. It was a wonderful visit. I gave Charlie my bedroom on the first floor of my house so that he wouldn't have to negotiate any stairs. He wanted to see the city, so we did the touristy stuff—the Kentucky Derby Museum and the Louisville Slugger Museum (Charlie was crazy about baseball and loved the Dodgers). We even had lunch at an *almost* authentic Italian pizzeria.

Charlie was an early riser, and early one morning during his visit we were sitting at my kitchen table. "What's your pain like, Charlie?" I asked. "You know, on a scale of one to ten, where would you put it this morning?"

"One to ten?" he responded. "It's about fifty."

At first I thought it was a joke, but then I realized Charlie wasn't kidding. He proceeded to take his medicines. I have never seen anything like this. Charlie had multiple pill boxes, three inches by three inches—one for each day. He poured out a mountain of pills, cupped them in one hand, and swallowed them with water in one gulp. When I asked, he identified every pill and what it was for.

At that moment, I prayed with Charlie and used a Scripture verse I had found highlighted in our mother's Bible. It was Philippians 4:13: "In him who is the source of my strength I have strength for everything." I got my mother's Bible and showed him the highlighted passage. We cried together, but they were happy tears. It was a sacred moment when we could feel the presence of our mother.

The next day I asked him if he had thought about his funeral. He told me that he had selected some music and some Scriptures. By this time, Charlie and his wife had joined a nondenominational church in South Carolina. It was very evangelical and had no rituals or forms of worship, so Charlie put the service together by himself. I asked him if he wanted me to be part of the funeral. He told me that he wanted me to attend and offer my own reflections and prayer.

He left the next day. We played phone tag and exchanged emails, and he sent me pictures of him at a Dodgers-Braves game. He got through

Christmas all right and seemed to be doing okay. One day in February, I said morning Mass, and at the end, as I usually did, I prayed for Charlie and my sister, Judy. When I arrived at my office, I discovered a phone message from Dale. I called her. "Chuck died this morning on the way to the hospital," she reported. I will never forget her voice. It was flat—as if the life had been sucked out of her.

She explained that Charlie had had one of his toes removed as a result of his diabetes. The doctor had prescribed an antibiotic that interacted with Charlie's medications for his heart condition and cancer. That brought on renal failure, but they had been able to stabilize him. He went home for only one night, developed respiratory problems, and died in the ambulance en route to the hospital.

It hit me suddenly how similar this was to the death of our mother. Charlie suffered through his various illnesses for nearly three decades, and my mother was a paraplegic for the last thirty years of her life. Like Charlie, during the last months of my mother's life she had relatively minor surgery, was hospitalized, sent back home, and then died of respiratory issues. It was so similar it really unnerved me.

I know this may be projection, but I strongly believe that a lot of my brother's strength in his illnesses was linked to our mother. They handled their sickness in the same way. They had an incredibly strong faith that God was with them. God was the strength they called upon to endure.

My brother, the miracle baby, the only child of my mother, carried both her diseases and her faith. I am convinced that God brings all things to completion at the end. If you can trust that, you can endure anything. I am still sad about their deaths and still miss them a lot, but I have no doubt whatsoever about their reunion in Christ's presence. That makes up for all their pain and suffering.

When sitting at the bedside of dying people, I am often amazed at the depth of their belief and faith. Even though I can't experience their suffering, I can understand how faith stabilizes them. For Charlie and my mother, it was never a question of why. They had a deep awareness of the passage from Philippians quoted earlier: "In him who is the source of my strength I have strength for everything."

At Charlie's funeral, people didn't talk about his personality as much as they talked about his faith. One ten-year-old spoke of how "Mr. Chuck" had given him a passage from Proverbs and told him, "This is your motto for life."

I know that Charlie is home—in the company of our parents—without pain or worry. He inspires me to keep my heart set on God too. I pray each day for a measure of faith as he lived it—a gift from God who loves us unendingly.

Reflection

My brother Charlie's life was an embodiment of the virtue of patience. Often people assume that a few persons simply are endowed with a greater capacity to be patient, as if it were in their genes. This may have been the case with Charlie, but I don't think so. The pain he endured, physically and emotionally, was intense. He lived through it with faith, a powerful conviction of heart and spirit that God was his strength; with God everything can be endured. He practiced the virtue of patience, knowing that his trust in God would be his strength.

Prayer

Lord, grant us the patience to seek and discover you in our daily life. Give us wisdom and trust that we may use your gift of faith fearlessly. Allow our strength to mature daily, confident that you never abandon us to a test beyond our capacity to live; in you we find our strength. As we suffer, we find you in our pain, broken and yet redeemed, leading us home to eternal life. Amen.

CONCLUSION

Listening to the Dying

An Interview of Paul A. Scaglione by John M. Mulder

Mulder: What have you learned from your ministry with dying people, and what has surprised you?

Scaglione: I began my ministry with the assumption that each person's dying was unique, that each one would have its own characteristics and dynamics. That has proved to be true. You can't escape the special qualities of each person's dying. At the same time, what really surprised me was the intensity of how a person made this journey alone and the intensity of my own feelings. I would be as close to them as I could be—emotionally and physically. I would assure them that I was there, that I was walking the path with them. I would hold their hands; I would bend over to put my ear next to their mouths so I could hear them whisper. I knew that I was very close with the person—physically, emotionally, and spiritually—but at the same time I felt a great distance. The intensity in that feeling of distance was a surprise to me, and that experience of deep intimacy and profound distance has always come home to me with everyone I have been with.

I've also learned that their journey is not just a pilgrimage of dying. It is a journey of many other elements of their life coming to some new conclusion because of their physical death. I used to think that if a dying person had a strong faith, they would muscle through it and bear the pain. That's partially true, but what I learned in being with people is that their dying is part of their living. Hosparus (or hospice) has a saying about the way you live is the way you die. I've found that to be absolutely true. The people who struggled the most in their dying had great difficulties with some of the most important relationships in their lives. Perhaps they were betrayed in a relationship, or maybe they were harmed by someone physically or emotionally.

What I learned is that when they would struggle with their process of dying, they would reveal to me more and more of their own vulnerability, their lack of trust, their woundedness. If they had lost confidence that they could find healthy relationships or that others could be trusted, then they often assumed that God couldn't be trusted either. Their struggle with dying wasn't because they were worried about dying. It was the end point of a journey that had begun long before I had ever met them.

Mulder: How did these struggling people affect you?

Scaglione: They made me unbelievably sad. I often found myself grieving their loss, and I would do that quietly and privately. If there has been an impact on me personally, it would be absorbing that loss for people. What I witnessed was a kind of unclaimed grief that they couldn't claim for themselves; instead, they described it as being betrayed or hurt by other people. I can't quantify this, but I know that sometimes I can feel that unexpressed pain, and I can absorb some of the reality they are going through. That has surprised me, and I never thought that was something that would happen to me in this kind of ministry.

Mulder: What do dying people say to you when they talk about God?

Scaglione: I think they're all trying to make sense of their dying. When I was in college, I read Ernest Becker's famous book, *The Denial of Death*. He emphasized that societies try to find meaning in death, and I thought immediately that the same was true for individuals. People seek meaning in their dying. The problem is that some people hold onto a belief system that isn't helpful to them. For instance, people may believe that if they hold onto an image of God as judge, maybe their suffering from this chronic disease or this terminal disease is partial judgment for what they have done or not done in their life. I wouldn't try to get people to reject such an image of God. That would violate them and wouldn't do them any good. Instead, I would hear the struggle and try to help them remember an experience or an image of a different kind of God that suddenly becomes more important and meaningful to them and gives them some solace in the middle of their dying. I find images of God changing a lot as people die.

Mulder: Has your image of God changed?

Scaglione: This is very personal because my understanding of God changed dramatically because of my near-death experience in a diabetic coma. Before that, I was comfortable with pretty formal ideas—for example, Jesus is the second person of the blessed Trinity. Coming out of my coma, I had a different sense, and I've used the image of insulin to describe my relationship with God. When I started taking insulin each day, I reflected on how a small amount, a very small amount, of liquid meant life instead of death. That made God much more particular and personal to me. Now God was involved in my ability to take this medicine and to use it in a conscientious way of caring for myself so that my life could continue. I started to have an image of a God who is very much a caregiver to me and has given me an opportunity to live. If God intends me to live, then there is a purpose in my life, and God is going to care for me and sustain me.

Care is the operative word for God for me, not *love*. I don't mean to demean the word *love*, except *care* sounds better to me. Caring is really how I understand who I am as a minister, and as a result, care is more important to me than what could be a very abstract notion of loving. When you think of caring and you think of people who have been kind and gentle with you, it's an image you know immediately, and you know the opposite too—when people have been angry and judgmental. So I think the concept of God that is most important is the idea of God as caring. I think it evokes memories of people who have been caring in your life, and those recollections become an inspiration for your thoughts about God.

Let me use an example. I grew up in a heavily Catholic neighborhood. All my friends were Catholics. There was a little store in the neighborhood, and it was run by Orthodox Jews. Here we were, this band of little Catholic boys running around, and we would always stop at the little store for candy. The Jewish couple were always so kind to us, especially the woman behind the counter. She would let us pick out our candy, and she would write down how much it was. Then at the end of the week, my mother would come in and pay for the candy I had bought. That would never happen today, but in my memory, that Jewish couple were people who cared.

Mulder: Did your diabetic coma also change your ideas about death?

Scaglione: Interestingly, what happened to me is that from the moment of my near-death experience, death in my life became less of a concept and much more of a sense of transition to an unknown. That is the metaphor I have for dying well. It is coming up to the point in your struggle where you go through it; you meet it head on. It can be overwhelmingly dark, but when you come out the other side, you are different.

And it isn't linear; it's cyclical. My life was always in God from the very beginning of my being created, and my life has never and will never be separate from God. I can go through experiences of darkness, suffering, and pain so that I can understand and come out at the other end—deeper in my relationship with God. I think that people who are able to go through that experience recognize that something fundamentally changes about God. God is not abstract, but personal. God is not distant, but caring.

Mulder: Do dying people talk about hell?

Scaglione: Practically never. They might talk about the concept of being judged, but I can't really remember many people even using the word *hell*. They might believe that they have done something in their life that has been atrocious and that somehow their dying, or the way in which they are dying, was a consequence of that. But I don't hear them speaking about eternal damnation and hell.

Mulder: What do you say to people who feel a deep sense of God's judgment?

Scaglione: There are people who are locked into a part of their life that is in the past, and they can't escape it. I can be with that person and give them some safe space where they might want to talk about it. But sometimes they can't even do that.

I don't think that God makes judgments upon us. I think that God ultimately wants to bring us to a place of understanding that he is with us. Even when we are judging ourselves or feeling guilty about things that we might have done or could have done better, God is there. So if a person is feeling guilty, I would try to ask them, "Where is the God who loves you or cares for you in this moment? Maybe God is different than you might imagine." If they can make any progress on that question, then there might be some reconciliation with themselves and their past experience. God can be there for them in a healing way. I try to ask if there is more here that they haven't looked at or experienced or attempted to know. Because I believe there always is.

Mulder: What about heaven? Do they ever talk about that?

Scaglione: It's very interesting. Dying people almost never talk about heaven as union with God. Instead, they often talk about it as a reunion with those who have died before them and who are in the company of God.

I find that really refreshing because it captures the Christian tradition's idea of the communion of the saints. John Paul II put it perfectly. About five or six years before he died, he flat out said that heaven is not a place. It's all about relationships and being reunited with others.

I think that is upsetting to a lot of people because they worry: "Who will I see and how will I relate to them?" So, I ask them, "How do you think you will relate?" Then they might say, "Well, my mother was a great gardener, and when I was a kid, she would teach me how to garden." I might say, "Maybe that is how you are going to connect." They might respond, "Oh, really? You really think that? Do you think that is possible?" And I would say, "Why wouldn't it be possible? What would prevent that from happening?" That always kind of stumps them and at least gets them to think about it and how maybe it might be true.

Mulder: Is there a difference between believers and nonbelievers in facing death?

Scaglione: I have to say that nearly all my ministry has been with people who have had a formal relationship with a religious entity. They have been Catholic or Protestant and in some cases Jewish. So it's impossible for me to compare how believers face death to how nonbelievers confront their dying.

There's a popular assumption that all believers face the moment of their dying in the same way, but that's not true. I find a wide diversity in how believers confront their dying and death. Even though they have been part of formal church structures, they are led to ask questions that maybe their church experience hasn't addressed or answered. I find people struggling with the human experience of dying. They see all of this coming to an end and they ask, "What is the purpose of all this?" Sometimes they might say, "I know I'm going to a better place." Caregivers often say that about the dying. Well, how do they know that? That may be their image and hope and desire, but they are imposing that on the other person.

I find that what most people find helpful in terms of religion is the sense of connectedness to others and to God. Somehow that connectedness makes material sense to them in terms of their dying. You can get the gamut from liberal to conservative ways of describing that connection, but when you peel away all the theology, what you find is that relationships are primary.

So even though I have not had much experience in ministering to non-believers, I would guess that the same dynamic operates across the board. It is a human dynamic and this is how we are as human beings. What we crave are relationships, and it is through relationships that we find meaning.

Mulder: Do believers fear death?

Scaglione: I think that for believers, the fear of death revolves around a couple of different things. One is simply the unknown of dying. I have been amazed at how people who are very faithful believers and very devoted to their faith and the church will say the same thing as they get closer to their death. They don't talk about their fear of death; instead, they describe their wonder about the abyss of an unknown. I don't particularly like the word *fear*. When people confront death, they don't know what it will bring, and they hesitate. They wonder; they try to figure out what will happen when they are touched by death.

Apprehension is really a better word. The apprehension of the unknown is primarily where people come to the point where they say that they trust that their not knowing is okay. They trust that somehow God is going to bring this into some kind of order that they can understand, so they are going to let go of their need to understand. I don't know that it makes them less fearful or apprehensive about the unknown, but I think it goes back to relationships. They become more firmly rooted in trusting God at that moment to lead them through their own dying.

The other fear about death that some people carry is the fear of enduring physical pain. That is very real. When you listen to them, it is clear they are worried that pain medication can lessen their ability to be aware and responsive to people. That becomes a struggle in itself because they want to hold onto their ability to communicate, which is one of the last places of control. Perhaps they have seen someone die in a great deal of pain, and they don't want that either. So they're torn. They want to remain alert and alive to others, but they are frightened of the pain that might accompany their dying.

Mulder: What about people who are angry about death?

Scaglione: Anger is a basic human emotion. You don't get angry over something that is inconsequential in your life. You only get angry over something that is valuable to you. Uncovering that valuable piece of life can be very threatening, and losing that piece or the threat of losing it is what makes people angry. Some people can be quite clear about their anger with God or with other people, but when you actually push them to be more reflective about their anger, that is a hard struggle.

Anger is also very complicated. I remember one man who was very angry with God. But he was especially angry with everything he had done in his life and the way people had told him how much he had done for the benefit of others. As he got closer to his death, he started talking to me about that and telling me how it was so much junk. I heard him devaluing it so that he could lose it. I didn't say that to him, but that is how it felt to me. People frequently devalue something in an effort to let go of what was really the most valuable part of their lives.

Rarely have I met a person who has dealt with their anger, particularly toward God, in a really redemptive way. Intellectually they might say it's okay to be angry with God, but I'm always left with the sense of "what else is going on here?" If people can articulate what is really going on in their anger with God or people in their lives, then they can make progress. If they can't do that, then they remain locked into their feelings of resentment. Unfortunately, that anger often gets plastered on other people, and that's very painful to see.

Mulder: What about people who are dying and are angry with others?

Scaglione: People who have had conflicts in their lives frequently ask, "Am I going to meet them there?" I have to say, "Yes, it is probably going to happen, and what do you think that will be like for you?" That is a struggle for a lot of people because they don't know if they are ready for that at all. I will often ask them, "What do you think might need attention so that you can meet that person face to face in the company of God?" That often gives them a chance to be honest and confront these conflicts by describing them and even resolving them for themselves.

I have often encouraged people to understand that when we are in the company of God, we will be with God as God has been with us. God has always seen us, so we will be able to see each other through the prism of God. We will see each other through God's grace and God's love.

Mulder: That raises a question about one of the stories in this book. It's the one about a woman who was abused by her father and her husband. If we are restored to relationships after our death, what does it mean to be restored to people like that?

Scaglione: Maybe the word *restored* isn't right because you are not restored to that relationship. That would be the opposite of what would happen in a redemptive situation. I think what would happen is a healing process so that the relationship fundamentally changes to a different kind of relationship. My sense is that it would have to be that I would have the ability to interact with such a person in a way that never would have happened in my previous life. The redeemed part of life, I think, happens when I begin to see and understand the person, not in the memory of the pain or suffering, but in the redemptive way in which God has brought that person and me into the presence of each other and God. I will then see that person as healed, and I will see myself as healed and have an awareness of my healing. I will experience them not through the memory of my wound, but I will receive them in their redeemed state. They no longer will see me as someone who can be victimized or taken advantage of because they are no longer viewing me out of their sin.

My guess is that this is going to be some kind of miraculous event. It would almost be like being reborn in the relationship because it is so different from what we knew before. When we talk about the afterlife, it has to be something where all our relationships are ordered by God and where God has brought them to completion. If there are still relationships that need to be worked out, that sounds like hell to me. I would still be entangled with all of this pain and suffering and be in a place where power and dominance and all of those dynamics would still prevail.

You know, I think about this in terms of my own experience of being abused, and if I am in the company of the person who abused me, it cannot be with any of the unfinished business of that experience. It's going to have to be entirely different, and only God can bring us to that. I can't. So, I'm eager to see that happen because I know that I can't bring my place of being a victim to the place of eternal life. Then I'd be in hell. I can't imagine being in the presence of God without being healed and without others being healed. I just can't imagine that.

Mulder: When you are ministering to somebody who is dying, do you come in with some idea of what might be of comfort to them? If so, what would it be?

Scaglione: No, I don't come in with a preconceived notion. As a matter of fact, I do the opposite. As best as possible, I try to shake out of myself any assumptions about how things should be or could be. I know that a person's story is personally unique, so that even though an individual might talk about a common human dynamic, I know that it has a particular value and power for that person. If you don't move out of your own world of assumptions, you end up listening with a certain level of judgment about how things should be and then making certain moves to make that happen. I think that's disastrous.

Mulder: How do you open up people's spiritual lives?

Scaglione: Often I ask people to start talking about the experience of God in their lives. I encourage them to be autobiographical and tell them I don't care where they start. It really is irrelevant to me because I want to listen. I need to hear their language and how they talk about their lives and about God. I encourage them to tell about important experiences in their lives and how God played a role. The more they can talk about their lives, the more they are teaching me their language and describing the world in which they live. Some people are better at doing that than others because I am really asking them to be very reflective about their lives. If we can get to the point of asking, "Where is God in what is happening now?" then we can reach a spiritual connection with one another and open up a relationship with God.

Mulder: What is involved in listening?

Scaglione: People talk about listening as an art or a skill. I don't think it's an art, and I think it's a skill you can learn. The temptation is that you try to apply the skill to all situations, and that won't work. So, in that sense, it's an art. Listening is a skill that becomes an art in its application. So how do you do that?

The fundamental starting point is to understand what is going on inside of you before you engage in a conversation with another person. You have to do more reflective work internally and ask yourself what are some of the assumptions that affect your ability to listen to another. If you are out of touch with your world of assumptions, your ability to accompany another person and to be with them in a listening mode is compromised. For example, if your loved one is dying, and if you believe this is going to be like your grandmother's death, you will miss what is actually happening.

But no matter whether listening is an art or a skill, it takes place in a relationship. That's the key. A relationship cultivates an experience of care, and that's how I learn how to listen well. Obviously, this means I am not judgmental. But it also means that every experience I have with another person will change my awareness of what it means to be a good listener.

I think of it as learning somebody else's language. I have always been bad at learning foreign languages, but listening is getting an ear for what someone else is saying. What's critical here is telling the other person to teach me the words. Admitting that I don't understand is very important, but even more important is my telling them I am eager to learn. This says to the person, "This is your story and I don't know your story yet but I want to know." You are inviting them to tell the story, and that is a great encouragement to people, particularly when they are dying.

There's also a deep theological truth here. It seems to me that the way we know the message of God is through a story in Scripture and the stories we tell each other about God's care.

Mulder: As they tell their story, is that an opportunity for you to link them with God's story?

Scaglione: Maybe at some point, but I wouldn't do that early on. I guess I would wait to hear how God is operating in their story. If they can give some idea about how their relationship with God works, then I might offer something, but generally that comes a lot later.

The fundamental thing that I have learned about listening to people who are dying is to make a connection with them without passing judgment. I will often hear a person give me a concept of God that I have rejected ages ago, but they are locked into it. I would never say to that person, "You need to get rid of that; it's a crazy idea." If you do that, you violate who they are as a person and you violate their struggle to come up with a concept that has meaning for them. For you to dismiss their idea is to say, in effect, your ability to come up with a conclusion is defective because it's not like mine. I think that is the most injurious thing you could say to a person. I might offer a person another concept that might be helpful, but I would never say they should replace their idea with mine. If I did try to replace their idea with my own, it would basically be saying that the relationship we are having here is about my giving you the right order of things, so if you would simply do it my way, you would be a lot better off. Well, how condescending can you get?

I think that is wounding a person at their most vulnerable point. If caring has any sense of meaning, it is because a person who is wounded and feeling very vulnerable knows you care when you don't lay any judgment upon what they are saying. That is exactly what they need. Caring is listening without judgment.

Mulder: What do you say to give a person hope?

Scaglione: That is a good question. I don't think that I would start a conversation about what I might give them as much as I would try to get a sense of where they have found hope in their life. What I have often found is that people will tell me about past experiences. They will reflect on maybe a relationship with a grandparent or a teacher in school or someone who was instrumental at some point in their life. They never lost the memory of that person. It is one of those turning points for them. I will explore that with them and ask, "How did you change because of that relationship?" They will often talk in terms of being inspired or having a sense about how good they really were or how they realized they had possibilities. Those are all things we associate with hope.

So I would ask them to go back to that moment. I believe that it is part of the Christian religion and tradition to always go back to understanding how God works in the history of our events. Those memories are not simply past memories or a pleasant past experience. They can be relived today. The best way of helping people come to a more hopeful place is to help them recall some of their own history and ask them how those moments of the past impact them today.

Now, I'll be honest with you that sometimes people struggle because at that moment of their lives they don't have a supportive and caring relationship. That is a real loss for them, and they are in the middle of grief in the midst of their dying. With them I listen to the grief, and I am always surprised about the depth of their grief over a loss that cannot be measured. If they can also recollect pleasant memories, that can make them more hopeful and inspire them.

But sometimes dying people are rejected by family members because of their dying. For whatever reason, the family members can't handle it, and they withdraw. You would hope that the opposite would be true, but sometimes the dying are abandoned by those they love. That is a difficult place. Those are the dying people I really try to hang onto because they need somebody who won't abandon them. Abandonment is a huge issue.

Mulder: Are there others?

Scaglione: I think the toughest one is simply loss. I hear about it over and over again. And it's true of my own life as well. The hardest struggle is letting go of the things that you have invested yourself in. I mean, how do you let go of someone you have loved? I hear that a lot from spouses. If I have been married to someone for fifty years and they are now coming to what we call the end of life, that loss is such a deep, deep loss. That is what people experience, and they don't want to let go.

Interestingly, right now I am accompanying a woman on her journey. She is not actively dying, but she is in the process. She says she is ready to die, and I think she is, but she is struggling with how do I let go of the people who I have invested in—my kids, my grandkids, and people who come to me seeking some wisdom and advice. She tells me, "I am not going to have that opportunity again." She is grieving the loss of that opportunity and the loss of her relationships. Even though dying people know intellectually that they can come to a sense of always loving others and that they will not be forgotten, there is a deep sense of loss. All relationships change as a consequence of people dying, and the finality of death is very real to people. It is a very difficult situation—especially because it is odd that God has said that it's relationships with others that are the heart of our lives. People get angry with God over this very issue. I have invested myself in these relationships, and now, God, you are taking me away from them. I understand how people can be righteously angry about that.

Mulder: What do you say to them?

Scaglione: I ask them to look at their life and ask themselves this question: What is the purpose of your life? Is the purpose of your life to invest yourself in the things that have happened in this life to the point that you would hold onto them forever? Dying is coming to the reality that life in this body is terminal. It is not infinite, it is finite. I always try to bring them back to that—because that is the reality. It is finite.

I also try to encourage them that as a believer, you know the truth of what C. S. Lewis says: It is not that we have a soul. We are a soul and we have a body. At some point the body dies because of injury or disease or other causes. We don't live forever, but we do live forever in a different sense, and that is what I call people to remember. We are connected with others and with God, and that connection survives beyond death. Now some people will say they believe that is true, but they believe it only theoretically. When they come into the great unknown, they struggle with their hope that it's true. But they confess they really don't know, and their fear of not knowing is where a lot of people get caught. I try to get them to ask whether they really believe they were created to be as they are in that body or whether there is a God-given life beyond that body.

Mulder: Do they ever ask about what happens to their body after they die?

Scaglione: That's an issue for a lot of people. "Will I have a body?" they ask. It's a particularly poignant question because as they die, other people are paying so much attention to their body. I frequently say to them, "What do you think about that?" And they will say, "I hope that I don't have this body." I will often tell them the stories of Christ's appearances after his death and assure them that their body will be some other kind of glorified reality that you and I can't really know right now.

But I will also tell them the story about my mother who was paralyzed for thirty-three years and lived in a wheelchair. Every time she would have a dream about herself, she was connected with her husband, my dad, and with her sister Jean, with whom she was very close. And she would always be walking just like any other person. So I encourage people to think of what their life is now and then expand that one hundred thousand times.

Mulder: What does Jesus Christ mean as you minister with the dying?

Scaglione: I would say that the thing that strikes me personally is that Jesus in his own death has linked himself with our dying. If someone who believes in Jesus looks at the death of Jesus for us, it is a voluntary death, and he chooses to die for our sake. But Jesus doesn't die just in order to accomplish something like salvation or atonement. That is how our theologies talk. I think Jesus dies for us so that he makes our dying sacred and so that we don't have to be threatened by the unknown of dying.

For me, Jesus' dying is a confidence and belief that as I pass through my dying, I do so in the company, support, and strength of the One who has died for me. So, it isn't a journey I make by myself. That is what I have learned by being with people of deep faith who are dying. They don't know that in any kind of formal or intellectual way, but they look at the cross and see the depth of the One who is love. Then death becomes less intimidating and frightening. They understand that God is with us through this experience, not separate from it.

Mulder: What about the resurrection?

Scaglione: Well, that is on the other side of dying. I don't know what it is. I mean, I really don't. I know all the images people have of it, but if God is with us as we die, then God will be with us on the other side of that death. Now, what will that look like? I don't have a clue. I don't know what that is like.

I am trusting that God made a commitment to us as our creator to be involved with us. Jesus affirms that, and through him God says that he is so involved in our human experience that he cannot separate himself from us. If God is intimately involved in the life, death, joys, celebrations, and everything of life, then God is going to be in the process of my dying as well. Personally I think that is what makes me more compassionate toward people in the process of dying because I believe God wants to share the journey of our suffering. If God wants to do that, then I want that caring to unfold and be real to people in their dying.

Mulder: From the stories you have told, it's clear that you pray a great deal with people who are dying, and you pray for them. What is the role of prayer in caring for the dying, and why is it important?

Scaglione: Prayer is fundamentally the language of the heart. It is the language of two people who truly care for each other.

This may sound strange, but I don't like to pray with people initially because I think you really need to build a relationship with someone before you pray. Since I am an ordained minister, people think I ought to be praying in formal ways, and I don't like that. I mean I do it, but the prayer I try to say is more the language of the heart and has a listening dynamic. If I can listen to a person talk about their relationship with God and where God has moved in their lives and where God has been important, I will often reflect that back to them in the prayer at the end of our meeting together.

I see prayer as a way of connecting the person, myself, and God in some kind of conversation. For example, if a person is struggling because they are afraid that God is going to judge them for something they have done in their life, I am going to use that as a starting point for prayer. I would pray that God would receive the fear of this person (and I always use their name) and would help them walk through that fear. That would be my prayer for that moment.

Other times it might be something the dying person says about a loved one. I would pray that God would be mindful of the loved one and that God would strengthen the dying person to be mindful of the one who is dear to them.

When I pray, I pray purely on the basis of what I have heard. I don't pray in an abstract way about dying, and I never pray for outcomes. I think that is bad. So-and-so is having a test on Tuesday and let's have a good outcome. That's atrocious. But I will pray that they will have courage in their experience of going through the diagnostic test and that they will receive it and have confidence in whatever the result might be.

The starting point for prayer is often where that person is, not where I believe they need to be. And when I say to someone that I will pray for them, I do not mean that I am going to go home and spend fifteen minutes speaking to God what God already knows. I do mean that they are not going to escape my awareness in my prayer. So whether that is in a formal way during prayer at Eucharist or in a personal prayer time when I am alone, I am going to be calling them to mind and remembering my conversations with them and above all my connectedness to them. It is not going to be a prayer for the outcome of a situation or a prayer that they have more strength. I don't pray that way. I pray more for a connectedness to the person, and so when I say that I will pray for you, it is that I am going to be very mindful about how you are within me when I pray.

Mulder: So the prayer that you would pray with someone is the same prayer that you would make about them? Is it a prayer that they could overhear and be comforted by it?

Scaglione: Yes, I don't think there is a fundamental difference. I think that when I say I am praying for you, I am basically saying that I am conscious of what prayer is.

What does it say in the Scriptures, that the Spirit prays in us when we don't have the words to do that, right? Why? Because it is the spirit of God that is motivating our prayer. Why? Because God cares. Why? I don't know why God cares. I trust that God cares because God's love is what compels us to participate in this very wonderful experience of God's care. This is the power of prayer: I am holding you here, consciously aware that God is asking us to connect with each other and with God. God is going to bring the outcome of the prayer to a conclusion that you and I might not know, but let's trust that and let's pray for each other, confident that God will bring us to the place we need to be. Whether that is a new awareness or whether that is an experience of a good outcome, whatever it is, whatever God unfolds, and whatever happens in the experience, God is with us. So if the experience of a diagnostic test is a bad outcome, as we would judge that, I still believe that God is there.

Mulder: You have spoken of things that ministers or caregivers shouldn't do. What should they do?

Scaglione: I think caregivers earn their stripes, even though "earn" isn't a good word to describe their devotion. Caregivers struggle with how to love themselves as caregivers even as they love the one who is dying. They often get lost in what they need to do for themselves versus what they need to do for their loved one. I encourage caregivers to be mindful of the fact that they can't give love if they don't have it within themselves. Their ability to love themselves or to take care of themselves is going to be more helpful to the person for whom they are caring. But that is much easier said than done, much easier said than done.

At the very end of my mother's life, she was suffering from an early stage of Alzheimer's and unintentionally began opening a wound on her body. I can remember standing at the foot of her bed. I was crying uncontrollably and saying over and over, "I don't know what to do!" I finally had to call the woman who was caring for her. What I didn't realize was the toll that my mother's care was taking on me and how little I was caring for myself as I cared for her. We caregivers tend to not take care of ourselves until we get to the point where we realize, "What more can I do? What more can I do?"

Caregivers need to know and remind themselves of how important it is to love themselves as much as they love others.

Mulder: What other advice would you give to ministers and caregivers?

Scaglione: It's extremely important for them to be very careful about how they speak about their relationship with the person who is dying. If you develop a relationship with the dying person, there is a confidentiality that has to be honored. For example, I would never discuss what I have talked about with a dying person's spouse without clearing that ahead of time. I think you have to be careful and honor the sacredness of the person's unique journey. I wouldn't carry any of that information to another person, no matter how close they were to the dying person.

People who are comatose are a special challenge. I try to help everyone around an unconscious person to recognize that hearing is one of the last senses that is lost and touch is the other. I would always encourage family members not to assume that because a person can't respond, the conversations aren't meaningful to the unconscious person. In fact, I believe the opposite is true. I think that not only can a person often hear what is happening, but they often desire to hear things that are important to them. They are making their journey away from this life, and I encourage people to speak to the person about their deepest feelings and desires and the heartfelt story they would like to offer and speak to them.

I often find that the people who struggle with dying are people who are waiting to have someone speak to them. It could be a child, a parent, a spouse, a friend. They want to hear that voice, and they are not going to pass easily until they hear that voice spoken to them personally—not in a group and not as a part of a cacophony of other voices. And the caregivers and loved ones have to take the initiative. It won't be a request from the dying person. It will have to come from the loved ones—in quiet, one on one.

Touch is the other thing that lasts in the body and awareness of a dying person. Depending on the person and their condition, touch can be painful too, so we need to honor that. But when that is not the case, then touch can be a very powerful way of communicating care. Holding a person's hand, stroking their forehead and face gently, combing their hair—these are some of the things we would normally do for someone who is ill. What do parents do for a child who is sick? They will often comb their hair or put a cold washcloth on their forehead.

Touching and holding are very important because they connect you and you don't have to say anything.

But the most important thing for people who are caring for someone who is dying is to recognize that the dying person's journey is unique and special to them. Above anything else, dying people need to be reminded that they are not alone in that journey. They are not making it just by themselves. They will not be abandoned. God is with you, and we are with you to the extent that we can make the journey together, and God will bring it to completion.

I think that is the most fundamental thing about caring: you are not alone.

Mulder: What is your advice for dying people?

Scaglione: The very first thing that I would offer a dying person is that they have to trust, and they really need to trust that God is with them. I would keep zeroing in on that. If they are having any kind of struggle at all, then I would encourage them to ask for the gift of being able to know and trust that God is with them.

Then there's the issue of pain. For me, pain is the place where we can encounter God and one another. C. S. Lewis put it powerfully: "Pain insists upon being attended to. God whispers to us in our pleasures, speaks to us in our consciences, but shouts in our pain. It is his megaphone to rouse a deaf world."

If you can be with a person who is dying and allow them to express their pain and talk about their suffering, that is where they have contact with God. I think pain gives us an opportunity to connect with God. I believe pain gives us the opportunity to connect to Jesus in a way that allows me to know that he is with me right now. As he and I go through this pain together, something else is going to emerge that I cannot fully see, but it will be redemptive. That is where I think C. S. Lewis is right. Pain is the connecting point with God and with one another. If we understood this, we wouldn't have to avoid the pain. Everybody in hospice will tell you that pain can be managed as part of the medical reality. Pain does not have to be obliterated because in it we can find a new understanding of ourselves and our connectedness to God and to others.

I'd also encourage dying people to deal with any unfinished business they might have in whatever way is comfortable to them. I might tell them: "Write a letter, and if you want to write a letter and make sure that someone reads it after you have died, that's fine. If you want to have a private conversation with someone, that's fine." They need to be honest in offering to another person or persons whatever they are carrying that is unresolved. They need to give themselves permission to be honest enough to offer to another person their deepest thoughts, whether painful or joyful. And they should use the method that is most comfortable to them.

I also encourage dying people to keep their loved ones close to them at all times—whether they are in great pain or not, whether they're feeling miserable or not. I think caregivers have an instinctive way of being with dying people so that when they really love a person who is suffering, they can be with the dying person in a way that supports them and comforts them.

Often I am really practical and suggest that caregivers surround dying people with things that will remind them of goodness in their lives. If the person is like my mother and likes to garden, that might be plants and flowers. Many times it's music, especially music that the dying person particularly loved and enjoyed. The aroma of food can flash back a memory of a wonderful celebration that they associate with that smell. Anything that brings connections with what is pleasant should be part of the dying person's daily life.

Mulder: Is there such a thing as "dying well" or "a good death"?

Scaglione: I can only know this as an observer because I can't know anyone's experience of dying. But I can say that those who seem to die well are people who have been the most honest about their life. If they have been as transparent as they can be and enter into that kind of vulnerability and woundedness, I think those are the people who die well. If they can talk about the difficult or painful parts of their life, caregivers and I can enter into their experience and create a sacred space of candor and disclosure. That is going to be a good experience of dying for them, and for me as I accompany them on that journey.

I remember being with a woman when she died—when she actually took her last breath. I remember that for me and for others in the room, there was a deep, abiding sense of peace. For the person who has died well, I think that is the finest tribute to them and their final gift to us—indescribable peace. I can't prove it, but I believe it is true. And that is a great gift.

CPSIA information can be obtained at www.ICGtesting.com
Printed in the USA
BVOW01s1907241013

334598BV00007B/350/P

9 781610 977722